Foundations of Faith
Education for New Church Members

Student Guide

by Michael D. Bush and Zeta T. Lamberson

edited by Laura B. Lewis,
Richard R. Osmer, and
Amy S. Vaughn

Book design by Carol Johnson

Cover design by Sharon Adams

PRINTED IN THE UNITED STATES OF AMERICA

ISBN 0-664-50095-1

About the Authors

Michael D. Bush is pastor of Westminster Presbyterian Church in Mobile, Alabama. Prior to assuming this pastorate, he served as pastor of Trinity Presbyterian Church in Richmond, Virginia, and as interim pastor of two congregations in New Jersey. He is a graduate of the University of Kentucky, Union Theological Seminary in Virginia, Yale University, and is a Ph.D. candidate at Princeton Theological Seminary. Michael and his wife, Janellyn, are the parents of three children and are lifelong Presbyterians.

Zeta Touchton Lamberson grew up in Columbia, South Carolina. She attended Presbyterian College in Clinton, South Carolina, where she majored in Elementary Education and minored in Christian Education. She went on to receive a Masters in Religious Education from the Presbyterian School of Christian Education in Richmond, Virginia, in 1977. Zeta served churches in Virginia, South Carolina, and West Virginia as a Church Educator for ten years before enrolling in the seminary. She graduated from Columbia Theological Seminary with a MDiv in 1991. Since graduation and ordination, Zeta has served as the Minister of Program Coordination and Education at Peachtree Presbyterian Church in Atlanta, Georgia. While at Peachtree, Zeta edited *Stepping Stones on the Journey to Faith*, a guidebook for children, youth, and adults on the basics of the faith every Christian should know. She and her husband, Bill, have two children, Zeta Elizabeth and Bart.

Contents

Introduction

Welcome to *Foundations of Faith.* In this eight-session course we will cover the basic building blocks of what we as Christians believe. *Foundations of Faith* explores the Apostles' Creed, one of the primary creeds by which we confess our faith. This course is based on the portion of the *Study Catechism* of the Presbyterian Church (U.S.A.) that covers the Apostles' Creed. The *Study Catechism* was approved for use as a teaching tool for the church at the 210th General Assembly in June 1998. It provides commentary in question-and-answer form on the Apostles' Creed, the Ten Commandments, and the Lord's Prayer. The *Study Catechism* provides us with a distinctively Reformed and Presbyterian understanding of the Christian faith. It gives us a Reformed perspective on a creed that we share in common with both Catholic and Protestant churches.

Group Sessions

The group sessions are divided into three main discussion sections. The first is "What Does the Church Confess?" When we confess our faith we say what we believe publicly, and in so doing we commit our lives to it. In this section of the discussion each week, we will examine what it is that the church confesses in the Apostles' Creed. We will use the *Study Catechism* as a tool for understanding how the Presbyterian Church has interpreted the creed.

The second section is titled "What Do I Think?" The Presbyterian Church has always placed a high priority on having a reflective faith. It is important for the church and for individual believers to reflect upon what it is we believe, and to engage in a critical appropriation of those beliefs rather than a mindless and passive repetition of words we

1

have been taught. This section of the discussion cultivates a reflective faith. You will have opportunities to think, raise questions, struggle with implications, and make affirmations. Here the *Study Catechism* becomes our guide and conversation partner. The catechism serves as a springboard for serious reflection, criticism, and dialogue. Through the discussion, we hope you will be better able to construct and articulate your theological understanding of the faith we confess.

The third section of the group sessions is "What Does This Mean for Me Today?" Sometimes we think of the Apostles' Creed as simply a bunch of tired old words that we repeat mindlessly in worship. The truth is that confessing this creed will change the way we live. When we join as members of Christ's church and together confess the Apostles' Creed, we commit our lives to the faith we profess. Christian faith is not just an assent to certain truths; it is a way of life. In this section of our discussion we will explore connections between what we believe and who we are and how we live our lives.

The *Student Guide*

You may use this student guide in the group sessions for ready access to the *Study Catechism* questions and scripture references. It also provides material for you to use at home in preparation for the group sessions. You are invited each week to prepare for the group session through reading, reflection, prayer, and writing in a journal. This work that you do at home in the midst of daily life will make the group sessions more interesting and substantive. In addition, we hope that through these times of reflection and prayer, you will begin to build or strengthen habits of spiritual disciplines. Each of the eight sessions includes the following:

THE *STUDY CATECHISM*

Questions and answers for the next group session are included along with supporting scripture passages. Read through the questions and answers several times as you prepare for the group session.

REFLECTIONS

After reading through the relevant catechism questions for the session, read through the background information given. This section explores the catechism questions and answers in greater depth, explaining the theology and suggesting connections for faith and life.

This information will both fuel your own reflection and provide a richness to the small group discussions in the group session.

KEEPING A JOURNAL

Each session includes instructions for keeping a journal and blank space in which to write. You are invited to read through the catechism questions a second time and choose a sentence or phrase to reflect on throughout the week. In addition, some sessions have a second option for your journal, based on the content of the session. Ideally you will be able to set some time aside for your journal each day and will be able to use both options each week. If, however, time does not allow or you are particularly engaged by one of the journal activities, feel free to choose only one.

If keeping a journal and a time for personal prayer and reflection is a new practice for you, you may find the following suggestions helpful.

1. Try to find a general time that you can set aside each day for fifteen to thirty minutes of prayer and reflection on the catechism questions. This will help to make it a habit and not just something you squeeze in when you have extra time.

2. Think about what is a good time for you. Are you a morning person or a night person? Do you have half an hour just after dinner or before your children wake up in the morning? Look for where you could best add something like this to your life and try it out for a few weeks to see if it works.

3. Pick a place where you can be alone and free from distractions (such as TV, radio, and the telephone).

4. If you find that you are enjoying the writing aspect of your preparation time, you may consider purchasing a notebook to provide you with more writing space for your journal.

What Is God's Purpose for My Life?

The *Study Catechism*: Questions 1–5

Question 1. What is God's purpose for your life?

God wills that I should live by the grace of the Lord Jesus Christ, for the love of God, and in the communion of the Holy Spirit.

> *2 Cor. 13:13* "The grace of the Lord Jesus Christ, the love of God, and the communion of the Holy Spirit be with all of you."

Question 2. How do you live by the grace of the Lord Jesus Christ?

I am not my own. I have been bought with a price. The Lord Jesus Christ loved me and gave himself for me. I entrust myself completely to his care, giving thanks each day for his wonderful goodness.

> *1 Cor. 6:19–20* "You are not your own, for you were bought with a price."
>
> *Gal. 2:20* "And the life I now live in the flesh I live by faith in the Son of God, who loved me and gave himself for me."
>
> *Ps. 136:1* "O give thanks to the LORD, for he is good, for his steadfast love endures forever."

Question 3. How do you live for the love of God?

I love because God first loved me. God loves me in Christ with a love that never ends. Amazed by grace, I no longer live for myself. I live for the Lord who died and rose again, triumphant over death, for my sake. Therefore, I take those around me to heart, especially those in particular need, knowing that Christ died for them no less than for me.

> *1 John 4:19*   "We love because he first loved us."

> *2 Cor. 5:15*   "And he died for all, so that those who live might live no longer for themselves, but for him who died and was raised for them."

> *Rom. 12:15–16*   "Rejoice with those who rejoice, weep with those who weep. Live in harmony with one another; do not be haughty, but associate with the lowly; do not claim to be wiser than you are."

Question 4. How do you live in the communion of the Holy Spirit?

By the Holy Spirit, I am made one with the Lord Jesus Christ. I am baptized into Christ's body, the church, along with all others who confess him by faith. As a member of this community, I trust in God's Word, share in the Lord's Supper, and turn to God constantly in prayer. As I grow in grace and knowledge, I am led to do the good works that God intends for my life.

> *1 Cor. 12:27*   "Now you are the body of Christ and individually members of it."

> *Gal. 3:27*   "As many of you as were baptized into Christ have clothed yourselves with Christ."

> *1 Cor. 6:17, 19*   "But anyone united to the Lord becomes one spirit with him. Or do you not know that your body is a temple of the Holy Spirit within you, which you have from God?"

> *2 Peter 3:18*   "But grow in the grace and knowledge of our Lord and Savior Jesus Christ."

> *Eph. 2:10*   "For we are what he has made us, created in Christ Jesus for good works, which God prepared beforehand to be our way of life."

Question 5. What does a Christian believe?

All that is promised in the gospel. A summary is found in the Apostles' Creed, which affirms the main content of the Christian faith.

> *John 20:31*   "But these are written so that you may come to believe that Jesus is the Messiah, the Son of God, and that through believing you may have life in his name."

Reflections

What does God want me to do with my life? What is God's purpose for my life? What difference does it make that I am a Christian? How is my life different from others who do not know the love of Christ? What does it mean for me to have a relationship with Jesus Christ as my Lord and Savior?

Our study of the catechism begins at the heart of our questions as Christians. We have accepted Jesus Christ as our Lord and Savior but are not sure what effect that has on us. The catechism uses the words of the apostle Paul from 2 Corinthians 13:14 to respond to the first question: "What is God's purpose for your life?" The response: "God wills that I should live by the grace of the Lord Jesus Christ, for the love of God, and in the communion of the Holy Spirit."

LIVE BY THE GRACE OF THE LORD JESUS CHRIST

What does "the grace of the Lord Jesus Christ" mean? The word *grace* might bring to mind a blessing said at the table, a name such as Grace Kelly, or a graceful dancer. The grace of the Lord Jesus Christ is something very different and unique. It means that Jesus died for us. The catechism says: "I have been bought with a price. The Lord Jesus Christ loved me and gave himself for me." The grace of the Lord Jesus Christ is about sacrifice and love. Unlike things we buy at the store, we do not have to pay for this. It is a gift given by God to each of us. We do not and cannot earn this gift. All we have to do is ask for it and it is ours—freely given. Once we have accepted this gift, we have put ourselves in Christ's hands. "I entrust myself completely to his care." Giving ourselves to someone else involves a lot of risk, but it also brings freedom. Just as a small child trusts a parent to provide care and love, we trust Christ and live a life of gratitude for the gift of grace. The psalmist says it beautifully: "O give thanks to the LORD, for he is good, for his steadfast love endures forever" (Ps. 136:1).

LIVE FOR THE LOVE OF GOD

The love of God is an amazing thing. God loves us so much that God gave the only Son that we could live. God's love is seen clearest when the eyes of faith look upon the cross, the symbol of God's power over death. First John says, "We love because God first loved us." God's love is a love that never ends. The biblical story witnesses over and over to the power and constancy of God's love. Even when humankind continued to sin and turn away from God, God's love endured. There is nothing we can do to separate ourselves from the love of God in Christ Jesus. In response to that love we live as people who are loved. We want to share God's love with others. We share God's love not only with our friends and neighbors but also with the stranger and the needy.

LIVE IN THE COMMUNION OF THE HOLY SPIRIT

Knowing we would need a constant presence to guide us, God sent the Holy Spirit on the day of Pentecost to be "God with us" in the world. Through the Holy Spirit we are in constant communion with the Lord Jesus Christ. On the day of Pentecost, in response to the gift of the Holy Spirit, three thousand people were baptized and the church began (Acts 2). We too become part of the body of Christ when we are baptized into communion with the Holy Spirit. After baptism we seek to trust in God's Word by studying and learning more about the Bible. We share together in the Lord's Supper and are strengthened by it. As we grow in our faith we pray to God for help and guidance on the journey.

As Christians living in relationship with God, we become intimately related to all three persons of the Godhead. We entrust ourselves to Jesus Christ as Lord and Savior of our lives. We live for God because God first loved us. We live in daily communion with the Holy Spirit who walks with us daily and guides us.

Keeping a Journal

1. Reread each of the first five questions of the catechism. Choose one sentence or phrase to reflect on for the week. Here are some ideas:

   • The Lord Jesus Christ loved me and gave himself for me.

   • Amazed by grace, I no longer live for myself.

   • I entrust myself completely to his care, giving thanks each day for his wonderful goodness.

   • God loves me in Christ with a love that never ends.

   • I take those around me to heart, especially those in particular need, knowing that Christ died for them no less than for me.

   See if you can memorize the sentence or phrase you choose, or at least remember the gist of it. Let this phrase stick with you through the week. Include it in your prayers, think about it while you are in the car, and remember it in the midst of a stressful situation. Look for connections between the phrase you selected and the world around you. Perhaps a conversation, a TV show, a current event, or a situation at home or at work will remind you of it. Record your thoughts and observations about this phrase and others in the journal space provided.

2. In addition to these reflections, write a prayer of praise, thanking God for the grace, love, and communion God offers.

_____

_____

_____

_____

_____

_____

_____

_____

_____

_____

_____

_____

_____

_____

_____

_____

_____

_____

_____

_____

_____

_____

_____

_____

Who Is God?

The *Study Catechism:* Questions 6–14

Question 6. What is the first article of the Apostles' Creed?

"I believe in God the Father Almighty, Maker of heaven and earth."

Question 7. What do you believe when you confess your faith in "God the Father Almighty"?

That God is a God of love, and that God's love is powerful beyond measure.

Lam. 3:22 "The steadfast love of the LORD never ceases, his mercies never come to an end."

Song of Sol. 8:7 "Many waters cannot quench love, neither can floods drown it. If one offered for love all the wealth of [one's] house, it would be utterly scorned."

1 John 4:8 "Whoever does not love does not know God, for God is love."

Question 8. How do you understand the love and power of God?

Through Jesus Christ. In his life of compassion, his death on the cross, and his resurrection from the dead, I see how vast is God's love for the world—a love that is ready to suffer for our sakes, yet so strong that nothing will prevail against it.

John 3:16 "For God so loved the world that he gave his only Son, so that everyone who believes in him may not perish but may have eternal life."

Heb. 1:3 "He is the reflection of God's glory and the exact imprint of God's very being."

1 John 4:9 "God's love was revealed among us in this way: God sent his only Son into the world so that we might live through him."

Matt. 9:36 "When he saw the crowds, he had compassion for them, because they were harassed and helpless, like sheep without a shepherd."

Ps. 106:8 "Yet he saved them for his name's sake, so that he might make known his mighty power."

Question 9. What comfort do you receive from this truth?

This powerful and loving God is the one whose promises I may trust in all the circumstances of my life, and to whom I belong in life and in death.

Ps. 12:6 "The promises of the LORD are promises that are pure, silver refined in a furnace on the ground, purified seven times."

Rom. 8:38–39 "For I am convinced that neither death, nor life, nor angels, nor rulers, nor things present, nor things to come, nor powers, nor height, nor depth, nor anything else in all creation, will be able to separate us from the love of God in Christ Jesus our Lord."

Question 10. Do you make this confession only as an individual?

No. With the apostles, prophets, and martyrs, with all those through the ages who have loved the Lord Jesus Christ, and with all who strive to serve him on earth here and now, I confess my faith in the God of loving power and powerful love.

Heb. 12:1 "Therefore, since we are surrounded by so great a cloud of witnesses, let us also lay aside every weight and the sin that clings so closely, and let us run with perseverance the race that is set before us."

Rom. 1:12 "So that we may be mutually encouraged by each other's faith, both yours and mine."

Question 11. When the creed speaks of "God the Father," does it mean that God is male?

No. Only creatures having bodies can be either male or female. But God has no body, since by nature God is Spirit. Holy Scripture reveals God as a living God beyond all sexual distinctions.

Scripture uses diverse images for God, female as well as male. We read, for example, that God will no more forget us than a woman can forget her nursing child (Isa. 49:15). "'As a mother comforts her child, so will I comfort you,' says the Lord" (Isa. 66:13).

Isa. 49:15 "Can a woman forget her nursing child, or show no compassion for the child of her womb? Even these may forget, yet I will not forget you."

Isa. 66:13 "As a mother comforts her child, so I will comfort you; you shall be comforted in Jerusalem."

Matt. 23:37 "Jerusalem, Jerusalem, the city that kills the prophets and stones those who are sent to it! How often have I desired to gather your children together as a hen gathers her brood under her wings, and you were not willing!"

Question 12. Why then does the creed speak of God the Father?

First, because God is identified in the New Testament as the Father of our Lord Jesus Christ. Second, because Jesus Christ is the eternal Son of this Father. Third, because when we are joined to Christ through faith, we are adopted as sons and daughters into the relationship he enjoys with his Father.

Rom. 1:7 "To all God's beloved in Rome, who are called to be saints: Grace to you and peace from God our Father and the Lord Jesus Christ."

John 14:9–10 "Jesus said to him, "Have I been with you all this time, Philip, and you still do not know me? Whoever has seen me has seen the Father. How can you say, 'Show us the Father'? Do you not believe that I am in the Father and the Father is in me? The words that I say to you I do not speak on my own; but the Father who dwells in me does his works."

John 17:24 "Father, I desire that those also, whom you have given me, may be with me where I am, to see my glory, which you have given me because you loved me before the foundation of the world."

John 1:12 "To all who received him, who believed in his name, he gave power to become children of God."

Gal. 4:6 "Because you are children, God has sent the Spirit of his Son into our hearts, crying, 'Abba! Father!'"

Question 13. When you confess the God and Father of our Lord Jesus Christ, are you elevating men over women and endorsing male domination?

No. Human power and authority are trustworthy only as they reflect God's mercy and kindness, not abusive patterns of domination. As Jesus taught his disciples, "The greatest among you will be your servant" (Matt. 23:11). God the Father sets the standard by which all misuses of power are exposed and condemned. "Call no one your father on earth," said Jesus, "for you have one Father—the one in heaven" (Matt. 23:9). In fact God calls women and men to all ministries of the church.

> *Gal. 3:28* "There is no longer Jew or Greek, there is no longer slave or free, there is no longer male and female; for all of you are one in Christ Jesus."

> *Eph. 5:21* "Be subject to one another out of reverence for Christ."

Question 14. If God's love is powerful beyond measure, why is there so much evil in the world?

No one can say why, for evil is a terrible abyss beyond all rational explanation. Its ultimate origin is obscure. Its enormity perplexes us. Nevertheless, we boldly affirm that God's triumph over evil is certain. In Jesus Christ God suffers with us, knowing all our sorrows. In raising him from the dead, God gives new hope to the world. Our Lord Jesus Christ, crucified and risen, is himself God's promise that suffering will come to an end, that death shall be no more, and that all things will be made new.

> *Ps. 23:4* "Even though I walk through the darkest valley, I fear no evil; for you are with me; your rod and your staff—they comfort me."

> *1 Peter 1:3* "Blessed be the God and Father of our Lord Jesus Christ! By his great mercy he has given us a new birth into a living hope through the resurrection of Jesus Christ from the dead."

> *2 Peter 3:13* "But, in accordance with his promise, we wait for new heavens and a new earth, where righteousness is at home."

> *Rom. 8:21* "The creation itself will be set free from its bondage to decay and will obtain the freedom of the glory of the children of God."

> *Job 19:25* "For I know that my Redeemer lives, and that at the last he will stand upon the earth."

Reflections

What does a Christian believe? Answering this question is at the heart of understanding what it means to be a Christian. To believe in something means to put your complete faith and trust in it. A Christian puts his or her faith and trust in the story of Jesus Christ. To be a Christian means you believe that Jesus Christ came into the world as God's Son for the salvation of the world. Believing in Jesus Christ means believing in the gospel message, the good news of the coming of the Messiah. Through the centuries Christians have used a variety of statements to proclaim the basics of their faith. The Apostles' Creed is one universal statement of what Christians believe. Both Catholic and Protestant Christians use this creed to state the main content of the Christian faith. The Apostles' Creed is divided into three paragraphs explaining the three persons of the Trinity: God, Jesus Christ, and the Holy Spirit.

GOD'S LOVING POWER AND POWERFUL LOVE

The first paragraph of the Apostles' Creed talks about God. When we confess our faith in "God the Father Almighty" we are saying we have faith in God's loving power and powerful love. The truest manifestation of God's love for us is seen in God's Son, Jesus Christ. The Gospel of John sums it up this way: "For God so loved the world that he gave his only Son, so that everyone who believes in him may not perish but may have eternal life." Through the centuries people of faith have found strength in a God whose love was powerful enough to suffer the agony of the cross in order to bring us back into relationship with God. Scripture promises that in life and in death we belong to God. God's power reaches beyond the grave to hold us in the palm of God's hand forever.

GOD THE FATHER

God was the father of our Lord Jesus Christ. Jesus called God "Abba," an affectionate term for father. In today's world the image of God as Father is difficult for many people because of the sinful nature of human fathers. However, our relationship with God transcends all human realities. When we pray to God as "Our Father" we do not mean that God is male, nor do we advocate the domination of men over women. Scripture uses a variety of images—male and female—to explain God's love. In Isaiah 66:13, God says, "As a mother comforts her child, so I will comfort you." Gal. 4:6 reads, "Because you are children, God has sent the Spirit of his son into our hearts, crying "Abba! Father!"

"Why is there so much evil in the world?" The catechism voices a question that challenges each of us. The reality and enormity of evil in our world is undeniable, and yet we cannot explain or understand it. As Christians, however, we hold on to two central truths in the face of evil and suffering.

The first is God's promise "that suffering will come to an end, that death shall be no more, and that all things will be made new" (question 14). Jesus Christ's death and resurrection confirm this promise and give us a sure and certain hope that God will triumph over evil. And so, "in accordance with [God's] promise, we wait for new heavens and a new earth, where righteousness is at home" (2 Peter 3:13).

The second truth to which we cling is that God is present with us now in the midst of all evil and suffering. We are never alone. The psalmist writes, "Even though I walk through the darkest valley, I fear no evil; for you are with me" (Psalm 23:4). We cannot deny evil, or explain it, but we do not fear it, for God walks with us and comforts us. The catechism affirms our belief that "in Jesus Christ God suffers with us, knowing all our sorrows" (question 14).

Keeping a Journal

1. Reread the catechism questions and answers for this session. Choose one sentence or phrase to reflect on for the week. Here are some ideas:

   - A love that is ready to suffer for our sakes, yet so strong that nothing will prevail against it.

   - This powerful and loving God is the one whose promises I may trust in all the circumstances of my life, and to whom I belong in life and in death.

   - God will no more forget us than a woman can forget her nursing child.

   - In Jesus Christ, God suffers with us, knowing all our sorrows.

   See if you can memorize the sentence or phrase you choose, or at least remember the gist of it. Let this phrase stick with you through the week. Include it in your prayers, think about it while you are in the car, and remember it in the midst of a stressful situation. Look for connections between the phrase you selected and the world around you. Perhaps a conversation, a TV show, a current event, or a situation at home or at work will remind you of it.

Record your thoughts and observations about this phrase and others in the journal space provided.

2. Spend some time imaging a loving God. Think of the times in your life when you have experienced this love. Offer prayers of thanksgiving for the people who have demonstrated this love to you. Think about times in your life when you have experienced the power of evil in the world today. Offer these times and experiences up to God. Place them in God's control and release yourself of their power. Offer a prayer of thanksgiving to God for God's love seen in the life, death and resurrection of Jesus, and for the ways God is at work in your life.

_____

_____

_____

_____

_____

_____

_____

_____

_____

_____

_____

_____

_____

_____

_____

_____

_____

_____

_____

_____

Maker of Heaven and Earth

The *Study Catechism*: Questions 15–27

Question 15. What do you believe when you say that God is "Maker of heaven and earth"?

First, that God called heaven and earth, with all that is in them, into being out of nothing simply by the power of God's Word. Second, that by that same power all things are upheld and governed in perfect wisdom, according to God's eternal purpose.

Rev. 4:11 "You are worthy, our Lord and God, to receive glory and honor and power, for you created all things, and by your will they existed and were created."

Gen. 1:1 "In the beginning God created the heavens and the earth."

Heb. 11:3 "By faith we understand that the worlds were prepared by the word of God, so that what is seen was made from things that are not visible."

Question 16. What does it mean to say that we human beings are created in the image of God?

That God created us to live together in love and freedom—with God, with one another, and with the world. Our distinctive capacities—reason, imagination, volition, and so on—are given primarily for this purpose. We are created to be loving companions of others so that something of God's goodness may be reflected in our lives.

Gen. 1:26 "Then God said, 'Let us make humankind in our image, according to our likeness; and let them have dominion over the fish of the sea, and over the birds of the air, and over the cattle, and over all the wild animals of the earth, and over every creeping thing that creeps upon the earth.'"

Gen. 1:27 "So God created humankind in his image, in the image of God he created them; male and female he created them."

Question 17. What does our creation in God's image reflect about God's reality?

Our being created in and for relationship is a reflection of the Holy Trinity. In the mystery of the one God, the three divine persons—Father, Son, and Holy Spirit—live in, with, and for one another eternally in perfect love and freedom.

Luke 3:21–22 "Now when all the people were baptized, and when Jesus also had been baptized and was praying, the heaven was opened, and the Holy Spirit descended upon him in bodily form like a dove. And a voice came from heaven, 'You are my Son, the Beloved; with you I am well pleased.'"

John 1:18 "No one has ever seen God. It is God the only Son, who is close to the Father's heart, who has made him known."

John 5:19 "Jesus said to them, 'Very truly, I tell you, the Son can do nothing on his own, but only what he sees the Father doing; for whatever the Father does, the Son does likewise.'"

John 17:21–22 "As you, Father, are in me and I am in you, may they also be in us, so that the world may believe that you have sent me. The glory that you have given me I have given them, so that they may be one, as we are one."

Question 18. What does our creation in God's image reflect about God's love for us?

We are created to live wholeheartedly for God. When we honor our Creator as the source of all good things, we are like mirrors reflecting back the great beam of love that God shines on us. We are also created to honor God by showing love toward other human beings.

Ps. 9:1 "I will give thanks to the LORD with my whole heart; I will tell of all your wonderful deeds."

1 John 4:7 "Beloved, let us love one another, because love is from God; everyone who loves is born of God and knows God."

1 John 4:11 "Beloved, since God loved us so much, we also ought to love one another."

Matt. 5:14–16 "You are the light of the world. A city built on a hill cannot be hid. No one after lighting a lamp puts it under the bushel basket, but on the lampstand, and it gives light to all in the house. In the same way, let your light shine before others, so that they may see your good works and give glory to your Father in heaven."

Question 19. As creatures made in God's image, what responsibility do we have for the earth?

God commands us to care for the earth in ways that reflect God's loving care for us. We are responsible for ensuring that earth's gifts be used fairly and wisely, that no creature suffers from the abuse of what we are given, and that future generations may continue to enjoy the abundance and goodness of the earth in praise to God.

Ps. 24:1 "The earth is the LORD's and all that is in it, the world, and those who live in it."

Ps. 89:11 "The heavens are yours, the earth also is yours; the world and all that is in it—you have founded them."

Gen. 2:15 "The LORD God took the man and put him in the garden of Eden to till it and keep it."

Gen. 1:26 "Then God said, 'Let us make humankind in our image, according to our likeness; and let them have dominion over the fish of the sea, and over the birds of the air, and over the cattle, and over all the wild animals of the earth, and over every creeping thing that creeps upon the earth.'"

Isa. 24:5 "The earth lies polluted under its inhabitants; for they have transgressed laws, violated the statutes, broken the everlasting covenant."

Rom. 12:2 "Do not be conformed to this world, but be transformed by the renewing of your minds, so that you may discern what is the will of God—what is good and acceptable and perfect."

Question 20. Was the image of God lost when we turned from God by falling into sin?

Yes and no. Sin means that all our relations with others have become distorted and confused. Although we did not cease to be *with* God, our fellow human beings, and other creatures, we did cease to be *for* them; and although we did not lose our distinctive human capacities *completely*, we did lose the ability to use them *rightly*, especially in relation to God. Having ruined our connection with God by disobeying God's will, we are persons with hearts curved in upon ourselves. We have become slaves to the sin of which we are guilty, helpless to save ourselves, and are free, so far as freedom remains, only within the bounds of sin.

John 8:34 "Jesus answered them, 'Very truly, I tell you, everyone who commits sin is a slave to sin.'"

Rom. 3:23 "All have sinned and fall short of the glory of God."

Rom. 3:10 "There is no one who is righteous, not even one."

Rom. 1:21 "Though they knew God, they did not honor him as God or give thanks to him, but they became futile in their thinking, and their senseless minds were darkened."

Isa. 59:1–3 "See, the LORD's hand is not too short to save, nor his ear too dull to hear. Rather, your iniquities have been barriers between you and your God, and your sins have hidden his face from you so that he does not hear. For your hands are defiled with blood, and your fingers with iniquity; your lips have spoken lies, your tongue mutters wickedness."

Question 21. What does it mean to say that Jesus Christ is the image of God?

Despite our turning from God, God did not turn from us, but instead sent Jesus Christ in the fullness of time to restore our broken humanity. Jesus lived completely for God, by giving himself completely for us, even to the point of dying for us. By living so completely for others, he manifested what he was—the perfect image of God. When by grace we are conformed to him through faith, our humanity is renewed according to the divine image that we lost.

Isa. 65:2 "I held out my hands all day long to a rebellious people, who walk in a way that is not good, following their own devices."

Phil. 2:8 "He humbled himself and became obedient to the point of death—even death on a cross."

Col. 1:15 "He is the image of the invisible God, the firstborn of all creation."

Rom. 8:29 "For those whom he foreknew he also predestined to be conformed to the image of his Son, in order that he might be the firstborn within a large family."

Question 22. What do you understand by God's providence?

That God not only preserves the world, but also continually attends to it, ruling and sustaining it with wise and benevolent care. God is concerned for every creature: "The eyes of all look to you, and you give them their food in due season. You open your hand, you satisfy the desire of every living thing" (Ps. 145:15). In particular, God provides for the world by bringing good out of evil, so that nothing evil is permitted to occur that God does not bend finally to the good. Scripture tells us, for example, how Joseph said to his brothers: "As for you, you meant evil against me; but God meant it for good, to bring it about that many people should be kept alive, as they are today" (Gen. 50:20).

Rom. 8:28 "We know that all things work together for good for those who love God, who are called according to his purpose."

Ps. 103:19 "The LORD has established his throne in the heavens, and his kingdom rules over all."

Ps. 145:17 "The LORD is just in all his ways, and kind in all his doings."

Question 23. What comfort do you receive by trusting in God's providence?

The eternal Father of our Lord Jesus Christ watches over me each day of my life, blessing and guiding me wherever I may be. God strengthens me when I am faithful, comforts me when discouraged or sorrowful, raises me up if I fall, and brings me at last to eternal life. Entrusting myself wholly to God's care, I receive the grace to be patient in adversity, thankful in the midst of blessing, courageous against injustice, and confident that no evil afflicts me that God will not turn to my good.

Ps. 146:9 "The LORD watches over the strangers; he upholds the orphan and the widow, but the way of the wicked he brings to ruin."

Isa. 58:11 "The LORD will guide you continually, and satisfy your needs in parched places, and make your bones strong; and you shall be like a watered garden, like a spring of water, whose waters never fail."

Isa. 41:10 "Do not fear, for I am with you, do not be afraid, for I am your God; I will strengthen you, I will help you, I will uphold you with my victorious right hand."

2 Cor. 1:3–5 "Blessed be the God and Father of our Lord Jesus Christ, the Father of mercies and the God of all consolation, who consoles us in all our affliction, so that we may be able to console those who are in any affliction with the consolation with which we ourselves are consoled by God. For just as the sufferings of Christ are abundant for us, so also our consolation is abundant through Christ."

Ps. 30:5 "For his anger is but for a moment; his favor is for a lifetime. Weeping may linger for the night, but joy comes with the morning."

Question 24. What difference does your faith in God's providence make when you struggle against bitterness and despair?

When I suffer harm or adversity, my faith in God's providence upholds me against bitterness and despair. It reminds me when hope disappears that my heartache and pain are contained by a larger purpose and a higher power than I can presently discern. Even in grief, shame and loss, I can still cry out to God in lament, waiting on God to supply my needs, and to bring me healing and comfort.

Ps. 42:11 "Why are you cast down, O my soul, and why are you disquieted within me? Hope in God; for I shall again praise him, my help and my God."

2 Cor. 4:8–10 "We are afflicted in every way, but not crushed; perplexed, but not driven to despair; persecuted, but not forsaken; struck down, but not destroyed; always carrying in the body the death of Jesus, so that the life of Jesus may also be made visible in our bodies."

Ps. 13:1–2 "How long, O LORD? Will you forget me forever? How long will you hide your face from me? How long must I bear pain in my soul, and have sorrow in my heart all day long? How long shall my enemy be exalted over me?"

Job 7:11 "Therefore I will not restrain my mouth; I will speak in the anguish of my spirit; I will complain in the bitterness of my soul."

Question 25. Did God need the world in order to be God?

No. God would still be God, eternally perfect and inexhaustibly rich, even if no creatures had ever been made. Yet without God, all created beings would simply fail to exist. Creatures can neither come into existence, nor continue, nor find fulfillment apart from God. God, however, is self-existent and self-sufficient.

Acts 17:24–25 "The God who made the world and everything in it, he who is Lord of heaven and earth, does not live in shrines made by human hands, nor is he served by human hands, as though he needed anything, since he himself gives to all mortals life and breath and all things."

John 1:16 "From his fullness we have all received, grace upon grace."

John 5:26 "For just as the Father has life in himself, so he has granted the Son also to have life in himself."

Eph. 1:22 "And he has put all things under his feet and has made him the head over all things for the church."

Question 26. Why then did God create the world?

God's decision to create the world was an act of grace. In this decision God chose to grant existence to the world simply in order to bless it. God created the world to reveal God's glory, to share the love and freedom at the heart of God's triune being, and to give us eternal life in fellowship with God.

Ps. 19:1 "The heavens are telling the glory of God; and the firmament proclaims his handiwork."

2 Cor. 3:17 "Now the Lord is the Spirit, and where the Spirit of the Lord is, there is freedom."

Ps. 67:6–7 "The earth has yielded its increase; God, our God, has blessed us. May God continue to bless us; let all the ends of the earth revere him."

Eph. 1:3–4 "Blessed be the God and Father of our Lord Jesus Christ, who has blessed us in Christ with every spiritual blessing in the heavenly places, just as he chose us in Christ before the foundation of the world to be holy and blameless before him in love."

John 3:36 "Whoever believes in the Son has eternal life."

Question 27. Does your confession of God as Creator contradict the findings of modern science?

No. My confession of God as Creator answers three questions: Who? How? and Why? It affirms that (a) the triune God, who is self-sufficient, (b) called the world into being out of nothing by the creative power of God's Word (c) for the sake of sharing love and freedom. Natural science has much to teach us about the particular mechanisms and processes of nature, but it is not in a position to answer these questions about ultimate reality, which point to mysteries that science as such is not equipped to explore. Nothing basic to the Christian faith contradicts the findings of modern science, nor does anything essential to modern science contradict the Christian faith.

> *John 1:1–3* "In the beginning was the Word, and the Word was with God, and the Word was God. He was in the beginning with God. All things came into being through him, and without him not one thing came into being."

Reflections

In our last session we discussed the first part of the description of God as "God the Father Almighty." God is the God of loving power and powerful love. We see God's loving power every day as we look around us. For it is in God's creation of all things, including human beings, that God sought to bring life and love to God's world. We know God as "maker of heaven and earth." Scripture begins with the story of creation for in God's act of creation, we become part of God's plan.

GOD'S CREATION

God created by the power of God's Word. God said, "Let there be light." And there was light. God had a plan from the beginning of time, and through the power of God's Word, God created all things out of nothing. God's creation culminated in the creation of human beings in God's image. The catechism explains that "we are created to be loving companions of others so that something of God's goodness may be reflected in our lives." What does this mean? It means we have a lot to live up to if we are to reflect God's love in our lives. At a very early age we begin to look into a mirror and see what God created. Sometimes we like what we see and sometimes we don't. But we need to remember that we are created in God's image and are called to reflect God's love to others.

With the gift of being created in God's image comes responsibility. We are to show God's love to all of creation. In our world today this carries a big weight. We do not always respond to the earth's gifts with care and love. We are often wasteful and careless with God's creation. We have a responsibility to ensure that the earth and all its goodness lasts for future generations. What are ways you can show more responsibility for God's creation? In what areas do you need to rethink your use of the earth's resources? We are to become stewards of God's creation. A steward on a ship or a plane is the person who takes care of everyone—the one who serves. This image can help us as we think about our care of all of God's creation. We are to be taking care of every need of creation.

OUR SIN

We are created in God's image to reflect God's goodness, wisdom, and love and to care for creation. And yet we have each and every one turned away from God and fallen into sin. We were created to relate to God and others with goodness and love, but our sin distorts and confuses our relationships. The catechism explains, "Having ruined our connection with God by disobeying God's will, we are persons with hearts curved in upon ourselves" (question 20). We cannot fix this situation by trying harder, cancelling out our sin with good works, or being better than our neighbors. "We have become slaves to the sin of which we are guilty, helpless to save ourselves" (question 20).

We are helpless in the face of sin, but through Christ we are given hope and salvation. "Despite our turning from God, God did not turn from us, but instead sent Jesus Christ in the fullness of time to restore our broken humanity" (question 21). Jesus lived for others. He was the *perfect* image of God. "When by grace we are conformed to him through faith, our humanity is renewed according to the divine image that we lost" (question 21).

GOD'S PROVIDENCE

God created all things and therefore cares for all things. God's intention for God's creation is good. God takes care of the world with wise and benevolent care and brings good out of the evil that happens. Paul states it like this: "We know that all things work together for good for those who love God, who are called according to his purpose" (Rom. 8:28). This is what we mean by God's providence. Trusting in God's providence means we believe God watches over us, comforts us, strengthens us, carries us when necessary, and will finally lead us to life with God in eternity. We believe God alone is in control. Believing in God's providence means we can cry out to God when we hurt and know God hears us and will bring comfort.

Sometimes we see God's providence clearest in our darkest moments. For when we have nothing else to cling to, God is always there. Sometimes, however, despair and bitterness threaten to overwhelm us and take away all hope. At such times faith in God's providence reminds us that "my heartache and pain are contained by a larger purpose and a higher power than I can presently discern" (question 24). We do not always have to "put on a happy face" before God. The Psalms are full of expressions of doubt, grief, anger, and shame. God's providence allows us to "cry out to God in lament, waiting on God to supply my needs" (question 24).

Several years ago my life was changed forever by AIDS. Within the span of two years I lost my mother and only brother to this horrible disease. My mother had undergone a blood transfusion and had contracted the disease from tainted blood. Her diagnosis came in the late 1980s when many misconceptions of this disease still existed. Being a strong woman of faith, my mother chose to keep her illness a secret, afraid of people's response. Her decision was hard for me, but I lived with it. Still, I spent many hours crying out to God. Why my mother? Why now? Why does she not trust her Christian friends to love and care for her? Finally, in the last few months of her life she took a step of faith. She had come to a point where she had once again put herself in God's loving arms. She shared with her community of faith her diagnosis. She had decided she wanted to help bring good out of this dreadful diagnosis. In God's providential care the church embraced her and walked the last few months of her life with her. Today they have an active AIDS care group and continue to minister to others in her memory. Less than two years later my brother shared his diagnosis of AIDS with us. Because God had seen us through our mother's illness and taught us so much, we were able to walk with him in his last days as well. In my life I have seen God take evil and transform it into good. Have you seen God do the same? If you haven't, be ready. For one day God will surely show you God's love and care when you least expect it.

God's Grace

God's creation and God's providence point us directly to God's grace. The very act of creation was a gift of grace. God stays with God's creation. God does not abandon us. God is always seeking us even when we are not seeking God. Life itself is a gift from God; the ultimate gift of God's grace is the promise of eternal life. God cares so much for all of creation that nothing will ever separate us from God's love—not even death. God is with us in life and in death. That is the message of God's grace.

Keeping a Journal

Reread the catechism questions and answers for this session. Choose one sentence or phrase to reflect on for the week. Here are some ideas:

- We are created to be loving companions of others so that something of God's goodness may be reflected in our lives.
- We are like mirrors reflecting back the great beam of love that God shines on us.
- Despite our turning from God, God did not turn from us, but instead sent Jesus Christ in the fullness of time to restore our broken humanity.
- Nothing evil is permitted to occur that God does not bend finally to the good.
- My heartache and pain are contained by a larger purpose and a higher power than I can presently discern.

See if you can memorize the sentence or phrase you choose, or at least remember the gist of it. Let this phrase stick with you through the week. Include it in your prayers, think about it while you are in the car, and remember it in the midst of a stressful situation. Look for connections between the phrase you selected and the world around you. Perhaps a conversation, a TV show, a current event, or a situation at home or at work will remind you of it. Record your thoughts and observations about this phrase and others in the journal space provided.

Who Is Jesus Christ?

The *Study Catechism*: Questions 28–41

Question 28. What is the second article of the Apostles' Creed?

"And I believe in Jesus Christ, his only Son, our Lord. He was conceived by the Holy Spirit, born of the Virgin Mary, suffered under Pontius Pilate, was crucified, dead and buried. He descended into hell. On the third day he rose again from the dead. He ascended into heaven and is seated at the right hand of the Father. He will come again to judge the living and the dead."

Question 29. What do you believe when you confess your faith in Jesus Christ as "God's only Son"?

That Jesus Christ is a unique person who was sent to do a unique work.

Luke 3:21–22 "Now when all the people were baptized, and when Jesus also had been baptized and was praying, the heaven was opened, and the Holy Spirit descended upon him in bodily form like a dove. And a voice came from heaven, "You are my Son, the Beloved; with you I am well pleased."

Luke 12:49–50 "I came to bring fire to the earth, and how I wish it were already kindled! I have a baptism with which to be baptized, and what stress I am under until it is completed!"

John 1:14 "And the Word became flesh and lived among us, and we have seen his glory, the glory as of a father's only son, full of grace and truth."

Question 30. How do you understand the uniqueness of Jesus Christ?

No one else will ever be God incarnate. No one else will ever die for the sins of the world. Only Jesus Christ is such a person, only he could do such a work, and he in fact has done it.

Isa. 53:5 "But he was wounded for our transgressions, crushed for our iniquities; upon him was the punishment that made us whole, and by his bruises we are healed."

John 1:29 "The next day he saw Jesus coming toward him and declared, "Here is the Lamb of God who takes away the sin of the world!"

Col. 1:15–20 "He is the image of the invisible God, the firstborn of all creation; for in him all things in heaven and on earth were created, things visible and invisible, whether thrones or dominions or rulers or powers—all things have been created through him and for him. He himself is before all things, and in him all things hold together. He is the head of the body, the church; he is the beginning, the firstborn from the dead, so that he might come to have first place in everything. For in him all the fullness of God was pleased to dwell, and through him God was pleased to reconcile to himself all things, whether on earth or in heaven, by making peace through the blood of his cross."

Question 31. What do you affirm when you confess your faith in Jesus Christ as "our Lord"?

That having been raised from the dead he reigns with compassion and justice over all things in heaven and on earth, especially over those who confess him by faith; and that by loving and serving him above all else, I give glory and honor to God.

1 Cor. 15:3–4 "For I handed on to you as of first importance what I in turn had received: that Christ died for our sins in accordance with the scriptures, and that he was buried, and that he was raised on the third day in accordance with the scriptures."

Rev. 11:15 "The kingdom of the world has become the kingdom of our Lord and of his Messiah, and he will reign forever and ever."

Eph. 1:20–23 "God put this power to work in Christ when he raised him from the dead and seated him at his right hand in the heavenly places, far above all rule and authority and power and dominion, and above every name that is named, not only in this age but also in the age to come. And he has put all things under his feet and has made him the head over all things for the church, which is his body, the fullness of him who fills all in all."

Phil. 2:9–11 "Therefore God also highly exalted him and gave him the name that is above every name, so that at the name of Jesus every knee should bend, in heaven and on earth and under the earth, and every tongue should confess that Jesus Christ is Lord, to the glory of God the Father."

Question 32. What do you affirm when you say he was "conceived by the Holy Spirit and born of the Virgin Mary"?

First, that being born of a woman, Jesus was truly a human being. Second, that our Lord's incarnation was a holy and mysterious event, brought about solely by free divine grace surpassing any human possibilities. Third, that from the very beginning of his life on earth, he was set apart by his unique origin for the sake of accomplishing our salvation.

Luke 1:31 "You will conceive in your womb and bear a son, and you will name him Jesus."

Luke 1:35 "The angel said to her, 'The Holy Spirit will come upon you, and the power of the Most High will overshadow you; therefore the child to be born will be holy; he will be called Son of God.'"

Heb. 2:14 "Since, therefore, the children share flesh and blood, he himself likewise shared the same things, so that through death he might destroy the one who has the power of death, that is, the devil."

Phil. 2:5–7 "Let the same mind be in you that was in Christ Jesus, who, though he was in the form of God, did not regard equality with God as something to be exploited, but emptied himself, taking the form of a slave, being born in human likeness."

Question 33. What is the significance of affirming that Jesus is truly God?

Only God can properly deserve worship. Only God can reveal to us who God is. And only God can save us from our sins. Being truly God, Jesus meets these conditions. He is the proper object of our worship, the self-revelation of God, and the Savior of the world.

John 20:28 "Thomas answered him, 'My Lord and my God!'"

Matt. 11:27 "All things have been handed over to me by my Father; and no one knows the Son except the Father, and no one knows the Father except the Son and anyone to whom the Son chooses to reveal him."

1 John 4:14 "And we have seen and do testify that the Father has sent his Son as the Savior of the world."

Question 34. What is the significance of affirming that Jesus is also truly a human being?

Being truly human, Jesus entered fully into our fallen situation and overcame it from within. By his pure obedience, he lived a life of unbroken unity with God, even to the point of accepting a violent death. As sinners at war with grace, this is precisely the kind of life we fail to live. When we accept him by faith, he removes our disobedience and clothes us with his perfect righteousness.

> *Heb. 2:17–18* "Therefore he had to become like his brothers and sisters in every respect, so that he might be a merciful and faithful high priest in the service of God, to make a sacrifice of atonement for the sins of the people. Because he himself was tested by what he suffered, he is able to help those who are being tested."

> *Heb. 4:15* "For we do not have a high priest who is unable to sympathize with our weaknesses, but we have one who in every respect has been tested as we are, yet without sin."

> *Heb. 5:8–9* "Although he was a Son, he learned obedience through what he suffered; and having been made perfect, he became the source of eternal salvation for all who obey him."

> *Rom. 5:19* "For just as by the one man's disobedience the many were made sinners, so by the one man's obedience the many will be made righteous."

Question 35. How can Jesus be truly God and yet also truly human at the same time?

The mystery of Jesus Christ's divine-human unity passes our understanding; only faith given by the Holy Spirit enables us to affirm it. When Holy Scripture depicts Jesus as someone with divine power, status, and authority, it presupposes his humanity. And when it depicts him as someone with human weakness, neediness, and mortality, it presupposes his deity. We cannot understand how this should be, but we can trust that the God who made heaven and earth is free to become God incarnate and thus to be God with us in this wonderful and awe-inspiring way.

> *Mark 1:27* "They were all amazed, and they kept on asking one another, 'What is this? A new teaching—with authority! He commands even the unclean spirits, and they obey him.'"

Mark 4:41 "And they were filled with great awe and said to one another, 'Who then is this, that even the wind and the sea obey him?'"

Matt. 28:18 "And Jesus came and said to them, 'All authority in heaven and on earth has been given to me.'"

Luke 22:44 "In his anguish he prayed more earnestly, and his sweat became like great drops of blood falling down on the ground."

Job 5:9 "He does great things and unsearchable, marvelous things without number."

Question 36. How did God use the people of Israel to prepare the way for the coming of Jesus?

God made a covenant with Israel, promising that God would be their light and their salvation, that they would be God's people, and that through them all the peoples of the earth would be blessed. Therefore, no matter how often Israel turned away from God, God still cared for them and acted on their behalf. In particular, God sent them prophets, priests, and kings. Each of these was "anointed" by God's Spirit—prophets, to declare God's word; priests, to make sacrifice for the people's sins; and kings, to rule justly in the fear of God, upholding the poor and needy, and defending the people from their enemies.

Gen. 17:3–4 "Then Abram fell on his face; and God said to him, "As for me, this is my covenant with you: You shall be the ancestor of a multitude of nations."

Gen. 12:1–4 "Now the LORD said to Abram, 'Go from your country and your kindred and your father's house to the land that I will show you. I will make of you a great nation, and I will bless you, and make your name great, so that you will be a blessing. I will bless those who bless you, and the one who curses you I will curse; and in you all the families of the earth shall be blessed.'"

Ex. 6:4–5 "I also established my covenant with them, to give them the land of Canaan, the land in which they resided as aliens. I have also heard the groaning of the Israelites whom the Egyptians are holding as slaves, and I have remembered my covenant."

Gal. 3:14 "In order that in Christ Jesus the blessing of Abraham might come to the Gentiles, so that we might receive the promise of the Spirit through faith."

Jer. 30:22 "And you shall be my people, and I will be your God."

1 Peter 2:9–10 "But you are a chosen race, a royal priesthood, a holy nation, God's own people, in order that you may proclaim the mighty acts of him who called you out of darkness into his marvelous light. Once you were not a people, but now you are God's people; once you had not received mercy, but now you have received mercy."

Zech. 1:6 "But my words and my statutes, which I commanded my servants the prophets, did they not overtake your ancestors?"

Lev. 5:6 "And the priest shall make atonement on your behalf for your sin."

Ps. 72:1, 4 "Give the king your justice, O God, . . . May he defend the cause of the poor of the people, give deliverance to the needy, and crush the oppressor."

Question 37. Was the covenant with Israel an everlasting covenant?

Yes. With the coming of Jesus the covenant with Israel was expanded and confirmed. By faith in him Gentiles were welcomed into the covenant. This throwing open of the gates confirmed the promise that through Israel God's blessing would come to all peoples. Although for the most part Israel has not accepted Jesus as the Messiah, God has not rejected Israel. God still loves Israel, and God is their hope, "for the gifts and the calling of God are irrevocable" (Rom. 11:29). The God who has reached out to unbelieving Gentiles will not fail to show mercy to Israel as the people of the everlasting covenant.

Isa. 61:8 "I will make an everlasting covenant with them."

Jer. 31:3 "I have loved you with an everlasting love; therefore I have continued my faithfulness to you."

2 Sam. 23:5 "For he has made with me [David] an everlasting covenant, ordered in all things and secure."

Rom. 11:29 "The gifts and the calling of God are irrevocable."

Question 38. Why was the title "Christ," which means "anointed one," applied to Jesus?

Jesus Christ was the definitive prophet, priest, and king. All of the Lord's anointed in Israel anticipated and led finally to him. In assuming these offices Jesus not only transformed them, but also realized the purpose of Israel's election for the sake of the world.

2 Cor. 1:20 "For in him every one of God's promises is a 'Yes.' For this reason it is through him that we say the 'Amen,' to the glory of God."

Acts 10:37–38 "That message spread throughout Judea, beginning in Galilee after the baptism that John announced: how God anointed Jesus of Nazareth with the Holy Spirit and with power; how he went about doing good and healing all who were oppressed by the devil, for God was with him."

Luke 4:16–19 "[Jesus] stood up to read, and the scroll of the prophet Isaiah was given to him. He unrolled the scroll and found the place where it was written: 'The Spirit of the Lord is upon me, because he has anointed me to bring good news to the poor. He has sent me to proclaim release to the captives and recovery of sight to the blind, to let the oppressed go free, to proclaim the year of the Lord's favor.'"

Question 39. How did Jesus Christ fulfill the office of prophet?

He was God's Word to a dying and sinful world; he embodied the love he proclaimed. His life, death, and resurrection became the great Yes that continues to be spoken despite how often we have said No. When we receive this Word by faith, Christ himself enters our hearts, that he may dwell in us forever, and we in him.

Acts 3:22 "Moses said, 'The Lord your God will raise up for you from your own people a prophet like me. You must listen to whatever he tells you. And it will be that everyone who does not listen to that prophet will be utterly rooted out of the people.'"

John 1:18 "No one has ever seen God. It is God the only Son, who is close to the Father's heart, who has made him known."

Eph. 3:17 "[I pray] that Christ may dwell in your hearts through faith, as you are being rooted and grounded in love."

Question 40. How did Jesus Christ fulfill the office of priest?

He was the Lamb of God that took away the sin of the world; he became our priest and sacrifice in one. Confronted by our hopelessness in sin and death, Christ interceded by offering himself—his entire person and work—in order to reconcile us to God.

Heb. 4:14 "Since, then, we have a great high priest who has passed through the heavens, Jesus, the Son of God, let us hold fast to our confession."

John 1:29 "[John] declared, 'Here is the Lamb of God who takes away the sin of the world!'"

Heb. 2:17 "Therefore he had to become like his brothers and sisters in every respect, so that he might be a merciful and faithful high priest in the service of God, to make a sacrifice of atonement for the sins of the people."

Eph. 1:7 "In him we have redemption through his blood, the forgiveness of our trespasses, according to the riches of his grace."

Question 41. How did Jesus Christ fulfill the office of king?

He was the Lord who took the form of a servant; he perfected royal power in weakness. With no sword but the sword of righteousness, and no power but the power of love, Christ defeated sin, evil, and death by reigning from the cross.

John 19:19 "Pilate also had an inscription written and put on the cross. It read, 'Jesus of Nazareth, the King of the Jews.'"

Phil. 2:5–8 Let the same mind be in you that was in Christ Jesus, who, though he was in the form of God, did not regard equality with God as something to be exploited, but emptied himself, taking the form of a slave, being born in human likeness. And being found in human form, he humbled himself and became obedient to the point of death—even death on a cross."

1 Cor. 1:25 "For God's foolishness is wiser than human wisdom, and God's weakness is stronger than human strength."

John 12:32 "And I, when I am lifted up from the earth, will draw all people to myself."

Reflections

Who is Jesus Christ? This is a foundational question for every Christian. We will spend two weeks looking at the answer to this question. We must know the story of who Jesus was and what that means for us. The story of Jesus is found in the Gospels of Matthew, Mark, Luke, and John. These four books at the beginning of the New Testament were written to tell the good news of Jesus Christ as the Savior of the world. They were written with the end of the story in mind. They were not recorded until after the crucifixion and resurrection and do not intend to be biographies. Instead, they explain the incredible events of the life of Jesus and proclaim him as the Messiah and the Son of God.

TRULY GOD, TRULY HUMAN

The Gospel stories tell us of angels that came to Mary and Joseph to explain the miraculous birth of Jesus and to guide them in their care of Jesus. From the beginning we know this is no ordinary child; it is the coming of God in human flesh—the incarnation. Jesus was not God in disguise, the deity dressed in human skin. Neither was Jesus simply a very good man—the best ever—who had a special relationship to God. Jesus was both truly God and truly human. Truly God, Jesus "is the proper object of our worship, the self-revelation of God, and the Savior of the world" (question 33). Truly human, "Jesus entered fully into our fallen situation and overcame it from within" (question 34). Jesus reigns in power for us, truly God and truly human, even today. When we call Jesus *Lord* we are recognizing his power in the world today and his power in our lives.

GOD'S COVENANT WITH ISRAEL

In the Old Testament God made a covenant with Israel. A covenant is a promise to do what one says. God promised the Israelites that they would be God's people and that through them all the world would be blessed. From the stories of Abraham and Sarah through the exodus from Egypt to the Promised Land and the kingdom of David, God's covenant was renewed. Even the prophets in the days of the exile in Babylon promised that God's covenant was still good. No matter how often Israel turned away to other gods, God kept God's promises.

Through the years God provided three special groups of people to help the people of Israel keep their covenant. The three special groups were prophets, priests, and kings. The members of these groups were anointed by God's Spirit. The catechism provides good definitions of each of these roles.

Jesus Christ took on the roles of these three special groups and transformed them. It is important to note that in the transformation of these roles Jesus embodied God's loving power and powerful love by taking away the sins of the world and taking on the form of a servant. Jesus was not the political savior the people were looking for, but he was so much more. God's covenant with Israel was extended with the coming of Jesus. The original covenant was expanded and confirmed. It now included Gentiles as well as Jews. God's blessing was meant for all peoples. God's covenant promise is still true for Israel today as it is for all people.

God's covenant with Israel continued with Jesus Christ and continues today. God's commitment to God's people never ends. God's promises are always present for us. In today's world where commitments are often not kept for very long, it is sometimes difficult for us to understand a lifelong commitment. Have you made a lifelong commitment? Have you found it hard at times to keep that commitment? God always keeps God's promises. We can count on it!

Keeping a Journal

1. Reread the catechism questions and answers for this session. Choose one sentence or phrase to reflect on for the week. Here are some ideas:

   - Only God can save us from our sins.

   - Jesus entered fully into our fallen situation and overcame it from within.

   - When we accept him by faith, he removes our disobedience and clothes us with his perfect righteousness.

   - No matter how often the Israelites turned away from God, God still cared for them and acted on their behalf.

   - Christ himself enters our hearts, that he may dwell in us forever, and we in him.

   - Christ interceded by offering himself—his entire person and work—in order to reconcile us to God.

   See if you can memorize the sentence or phrase you choose, or at least remember the gist of it. Let this phrase stick with you through the week. Include it in your prayers, think about it while you are in the car, and remember it in the midst of a stressful situation. Look for connections between the phrase you selected and the world around you. Perhaps a conversation, a TV show, a current event, or a situation at home or at work will remind you of it. Record your thoughts and observations about this phrase and others in the journal space provided.

2. Reflect a few minutes on commitments you have made in your life. Are there some you need to reevaluate? Are there people to whom you need to make new commitments? Offer your commitments and your relationships to God in prayer. Ask for help in strengthening them. Reflect upon your relationship with Jesus Christ. Is it all it can be? Are there areas you need to explore deeper or seek help with? Offer them to God for guidance and help.

The Saving Significance of Jesus' Death

The *Study Catechism:* Questions 42–52

> **Question 42. What do you affirm when you say that he "suffered under Pontius Pilate"?**
>
> First, that our Lord was humiliated, rejected, and abused by the temporal authorities of his day, both religious and political. Christ thus aligned himself with all human beings who are oppressed, tortured, or otherwise shamefully treated by those with worldly power. Second, and even more importantly, that our Lord, though innocent, submitted himself to condemnation by an earthly judge so that through him we ourselves, though guilty, might be acquitted before our heavenly Judge.
>
> > *Luke 18:32* "For he will be handed over to the Gentiles; and he will be mocked and insulted and spat upon."
> >
> > *Isa. 53:3* "He was despised and rejected by others; a man of suffering and acquainted with infirmity; and as one from whom others hide their faces he was despised, and we held him of no account."
> >
> > *Ps. 9:9* "The LORD is a stronghold for the oppressed, a stronghold in times of trouble."
> >
> > *Luke 1:52* "He has brought down the powerful from their thrones, and lifted up the lowly."
> >
> > *2 Cor. 5:21* "For our sake he made him to be sin who knew no sin, so that in him we might become the righteousness of God."
> >
> > *2 Tim. 4:8* "From now on there is reserved for me the crown of righteousness, which the Lord, the righteous judge, will give me on that day, and not only to me but also to all who have longed for his appearing."

Question 43. What do you affirm when you say that he was "crucified, dead, and buried"?

That when our Lord passed through the door of real human death, he showed us that there is no sorrow he has not known, no grief he has not borne, and no price he was unwilling to pay in order to reconcile us to God.

> *Matt. 26:38–39* "Then he said to them, 'I am deeply grieved, even to death; remain here, and stay awake with me.' And going a little farther, he threw himself on the ground and prayed, 'My Father, if it is possible, let this cup pass from me; yet not what I want but what you want.'"

> *Isa. 53:5* "But he was wounded for our transgressions, crushed for our iniquities; upon him was the punishment that made us whole, and by his bruises we are healed."

> *Gal. 3:13* "Christ redeemed us from the curse of the law by becoming a curse for us—for it is written, 'Cursed is everyone who hangs on a tree.'"

> *Heb. 2:9* "But we do see Jesus, who for a little while was made lower than the angels, now crowned with glory and honor because of the suffering of death, so that by the grace of God he might taste death for everyone."

> *2 Cor. 5:19* "In Christ God was reconciling the world to himself, not counting their trespasses against them, and entrusting the message of reconciliation to us."

Question 44. What do you affirm when you say that he "descended into hell"?

That our Lord took upon himself the full consequences of our sinfulness, even the agony of abandonment by God, in order that we might be spared.

> *Mark 15:34* "At three o'clock Jesus cried out with a loud voice, 'Eloi, Eloi, lema sabachthani?' which means, 'My God, my God, why have you forsaken me?'"

> *Heb. 9:26* "He has appeared once for all at the end of the age to remove sin by the sacrifice of himself."

> *Rom. 4:24–25* "It will be reckoned to us who believe in him who raised Jesus our Lord from the dead, who was handed over to death for our trespasses and was raised for our justification."

Question 45. Why did Jesus have to suffer as he did?

Because grace is more abundant—and sin more serious—than we suppose. However cruelly we may treat one another, all sin is primarily against God. God condemns sin, yet never judges apart from grace. In giving Jesus Christ to die for us, God took the burden of our sin into God's own self to remove it once and for all. The cross in all its severity reveals an abyss of sin swallowed up by the suffering of divine love.

Rom. 8:1, 3–4 "There is therefore now no condemnation for those who are in Christ Jesus. For God has done what the law, weakened by the flesh, could not do: by sending his own Son in the likeness of sinful flesh, and to deal with sin, he condemned sin in the flesh, so that the just requirement of the law might be fulfilled in us."

1 Cor. 1:18 "For the message about the cross is foolishness to those who are perishing, but to us who are being saved it is the power of God."

Rom. 5:8 "But God proves his love for us in that while we still were sinners Christ died for us."

Col. 1:20 "Through him God was pleased to reconcile to himself all things, whether on earth or in heaven, by making peace through the blood of his cross."

James 2:13 "For judgment will be without mercy to anyone who has shown no mercy; mercy triumphs over judgment."

Question 46. What do you affirm when you say that "on the third day he rose again from the dead"?

That our Lord could not be held by the power of death. Having died on the cross, he appeared to his followers, triumphant from the grave, in a new, exalted kind of life. In showing them his hands and his feet, the one who was crucified revealed himself to them as the Lord and Savior of the world.

Acts 2:24 "But God raised him up, having freed him from death, because it was impossible for him to be held in its power."

1 Cor. 15:3–4 "For I handed on to you as of first importance what I in turn had received: that Christ died for our sins in accordance with the scriptures, and that he was buried, and that he was raised on the third day in accordance with the scriptures."

Luke 24:36–40 "While they were talking about this, Jesus himself stood among them and said to them, 'Peace be with you.' They were startled and terrified, and thought that they were seeing a ghost. He said to them, 'Why are you frightened, and why do doubts arise in your hearts? Look at my hands and my feet; see that it is I myself. Touch me and see; for a ghost does not have flesh and bones as you see that I have.' And when he had said this, he showed them his hands and his feet."

John 20:15–18 "Jesus said to her, 'Woman, why are you weeping? Whom are you looking for?' Supposing him to be the gardener, she said to him, 'Sir, if you have carried him away, tell me where you have laid him, and I will take him away.' Jesus said to her, 'Mary!' She turned and said to him in Hebrew, 'Rabbouni!' (which means Teacher). Jesus said to her, 'Do not hold on to me, because I have not yet ascended to the Father. But go to my brothers and say to them, "I am ascending to my Father and your Father, to my God and your God."' Mary Magdalene went and announced to the disciples, 'I have seen the Lord'; and she told them that he had said these things to her."

1 Cor. 15:5–8 "He appeared to Cephas, then to the twelve. Then he appeared to more than five hundred brothers and sisters at one time, most of whom are still alive, though some have died. Then he appeared to James, then to all the apostles. Last of all, as to one untimely born, he appeared also to me."

John 20:27 "Then he said to Thomas, 'Put your finger here and see my hands. Reach out your hand and put it in my side. Do not doubt but believe.'"

Question 47. What do you affirm when you say that "he ascended into heaven and is seated at the right hand of the Father"?

First, that Christ has gone to be with the Father, hidden except to the eyes of faith. Second, however, that Christ is not cut off from us in the remote past, or in some place from which he cannot reach us, but is present to us here and now by grace. He reigns with divine authority, protecting us, guiding us, and interceding for us until he returns in glory.

Acts 1:6–11 "So when they had come together, they asked him, 'Lord, is this the time when you will restore the kingdom to Israel?' He replied, 'It is not for you to know the times or periods that the Father has set by his own authority. But you will receive power when the Holy Spirit has come upon you; and you will be my witnesses in Jerusalem, in all Judea and Samaria, and to the ends of the earth.' When he had said this, as they were watching, he was lifted up, and a cloud took him out of their sight. While he was going and they were gazing up toward heaven, suddenly two men in white robes stood by them. They said, 'Men of Galilee, why do you stand looking up toward heaven? This Jesus, who has been taken up from you into heaven, will come in the same way as you saw him go into heaven.'"

Col. 3:1 "So if you have been raised with Christ, seek the things that are above, where Christ is, seated at the right hand of God."

Question 48. How do you understand the words that "he will come again to judge the living and the dead"?

Like everyone else, I too must stand in fear and trembling before the judgment seat of Christ. But the Judge is the one who submitted to judgment for my sake. Nothing will be able to separate me from the love of God in Christ Jesus my Lord. All the sinful failures that cause me shame will perish as through fire, while any good I may have done will be received with gladness by God.

2 Cor. 5:10 "For all of us must appear before the judgment seat of Christ, so that each may receive recompense for what has been done in the body, whether good or evil."

Eccl. 12:14 "For God will bring every deed into judgment, including every secret thing, whether good or evil."

Acts 17:31 "He has fixed a day on which he will have the world judged in righteousness by a man whom he has appointed, and of this he has given assurance to all by raising him from the dead."

Rom. 8:38–39 "For I am convinced that neither death, nor life, nor angels, nor rulers, nor things present, nor things to come, nor powers, nor height, nor depth, nor anything else in all creation, will be able to separate us from the love of God in Christ Jesus our Lord."

1 John 4:17 "Love has been perfected among us in this: that we may have boldness on the day of judgment, because as he is, so are we in this world."

1 Cor. 3:12–15 "Now if anyone builds on the foundation with gold, silver, precious stones, wood, hay, straw—the work of each builder will become visible, for the Day will disclose it, because it will be revealed with fire, and the fire will test what sort of work each has done. If what has been built on the foundation survives, the builder will receive a reward. If the work is burned up, the builder will suffer loss; the builder will be saved, but only as through fire."

Acts 10:42 "He is the one ordained by God as judge of the living and the dead."

Question 49. Will all human beings be saved?

No one will be lost who can be saved. The limits to salvation, whatever they may be, are known only to God. Three truths above all are certain. God is a holy God who is not to be trifled with. No one will be saved except by grace alone. And no judge could possibly be more gracious than our Lord and Savior, Jesus Christ.

Heb 10:31 "It is a fearful thing to fall into the hands of the living God."

Rom. 11:32 "For God has imprisoned all in disobedience so that he may be merciful to all."

Matt. 18:12–14 "What do you think? If a shepherd has a hundred sheep, and one of them has gone astray, does he not leave the ninety-nine on the mountains and go in search of the one that went astray? And if he finds it, truly I tell you, he rejoices over it more than over the ninety-nine that never went astray. So it is not the will of your Father in heaven that one of these little ones should be lost."

Eph. 2:8 "For by grace you have been saved through faith, and this is not your own doing; it is the gift of God."

1 Tim. 2:3–4 "This is right and is acceptable in the sight of God our Savior, who desires everyone to be saved and to come to the knowledge of the truth."

John 3:17–18 "Indeed, God did not send the Son into the world to condemn the world, but in order that the world might be saved through him. Those who believe in him are not condemned; but those who do not believe are condemned already, because they have not believed in the name of the only Son of God."

Ezek. 18:32 "For I have no pleasure in the death of anyone, says the Lord GOD. Turn, then, and live."

2 Cor. 5:14–15 "For the love of Christ urges us on, because we are convinced that one has died for all; therefore all have died. And he died for all, so that those who live might live no longer for themselves, but for him who died and was raised for them."

Question 50. Is Christianity the only true religion?

Religion is a complex matter. When used as a means to promote self-justification, war-mongering, or prejudice, it is a form of sin. Too often all religions—and not least Christianity—have been twisted in this way. Nevertheless, by grace, despite all disobedience, Christianity offers the truth of the gospel. Although other religions may enshrine various truths, no other can or does affirm the name of Jesus Christ as the hope of the world.

Matt 7:3 "Why do you see the speck in your neighbor's eye, but do not notice the log in your own eye?"

James 1:26 "If any think they are religious, and do not bridle their tongues but deceive their hearts, their religion is worthless."

James 1:27 "Religion that is pure and undefiled before God, the Father, is this: to care for orphans and widows in their distress, and to keep oneself unstained by the world."

Acts 4:12 "There is salvation in no one else, for there is no other name under heaven given among mortals by which we must be saved."

John 14:6 "Jesus said to him, 'I am the way, and the truth, and the life. No one comes to the Father except through me.'"

Rom. 1:16 "For I am not ashamed of the gospel; it is the power of God for salvation to everyone who has faith, to the Jew first and also to the Greek."

2 Cor. 4:7 "But we have this treasure in clay jars, so that it may be made clear that this extraordinary power belongs to God and does not come from us."

Question 51. How will God deal with the followers of other religions?

God has made salvation available to all human beings through Jesus Christ, crucified and risen. How God will deal with those who do not know or follow Christ, but who follow another tradition, we cannot finally say. We can say, however, that God is gracious and merciful, and that God will not deal with people in any other way than we see in Jesus Christ, who came as the Savior of the world.

Rev. 7:9 "And there was a great multitude that no one could count, from every nation, from all tribes and peoples and languages, standing before the throne and before the Lamb, robed in white, with palm branches in their hands."

Ps. 103:8 "The LORD is merciful and gracious, slow to anger and abounding in steadfast love."

John 3:19   "And this is the judgment, that the light has come into the world, and people loved darkness rather than light because their deeds were evil."

Titus 2:11   "For the grace of God has appeared, bringing salvation to all."

Question 52. How should I treat non-Christians and people of other religions?

As much as I can, I should meet friendship with friendship, hostility with kindness, generosity with gratitude, persecution with forbearance, truth with agreement, and error with truth. I should express my faith with humility and devotion as the occasion requires, whether silently or openly, boldly or meekly, by word or by deed. I should avoid compromising the truth on the one hand and being narrow-minded on the other. In short, I should always welcome and accept these others in a way that honors and reflects the Lord's welcome and acceptance of me.

Rom. 15:7   "Welcome one another, therefore, just as Christ has welcomed you, for the glory of God."

Luke 6:37   "Do not judge, and you will not be judged; do not condemn, and you will not be condemned. Forgive, and you will be forgiven."

Matt. 5:44   "But I say to you, Love your enemies and pray for those who persecute you."

Eph. 4:25   "So then, putting away falsehood, let all of us speak the truth to our neighbors, for we are members of one another."

Acts 13:47   "For so the Lord has commanded us, saying, 'I have set you to be a light for the Gentiles, so that you may bring salvation to the ends of the earth.'"

Rom. 12:21   "Do not be overcome by evil, but overcome evil with good."

Rom. 13:10   "Love does no wrong to a neighbor; therefore, love is the fulfilling of the law."

Reflections

What difference does the death and resurrection of Jesus Christ make? What does it mean to say Jesus is Lord and Savior? What does it mean to be saved? Who will be saved? What do I have to do to be saved? How will my life be different? All of these are questions at the heart of Christianity. This section of the catechism deals with these central questions of our faith.

Knowing Who Jesus Is

The heart of the gospel is found in the story of the death and resurrection of Jesus. To understand the gospel we need to know the sequence of events that led up to this event. All four Gospels tell the story. Read the events from Palm Sunday through the Resurrection in one of the Gospels: Matthew 21:1–28:20; Mark 11:1–16:20; Luke 19:28–24:53; John 12:12–21:25.

Years before, the prophet Isaiah spoke of a suffering servant who would come and "bear our griefs" (Isa. 53:2–12). When we compare the events of the last week of Jesus' life with the prophet's message, we believe Jesus Christ fulfilled the longing for a messiah who was also a suffering servant.

The power of the story of the death and resurrection of Jesus is seen in the witness over the past two thousand years to these events. God sent Jesus into the world for each of us. God loved us so much God was willing to sacrifice God's Son that we might have a new life. We proclaim this message when we profess our faith in Jesus Christ as Lord and Savior. The first question asked when you join a Presbyterian Church is "Who is your Lord and Savior?" What does it mean to say Jesus is our Lord and Savior?

Jesus as Lord and Savior

When we proclaim Jesus as Lord we share in Peter's Pentecost affirmation that Jesus was God's Son: "Let the entire house of Israel know with certainty that God has made him both Lord and Messiah, this Jesus whom you crucified" (Acts 2:36). Catechism questions 29–31 dealt specifically with this message.

Because of Jesus' suffering and death on the cross we respond by proclaiming Jesus Christ as Lord. In his letter to the Philippians, Paul proclaims this clearly in the great Christ hymn: "At the name of Jesus every knee should bend, in heaven and on earth and under the earth, and every tongue should confess that Jesus Christ is Lord, to the glory of God the Father" (Phil 2:10–11).

The catechism does not treat the significance of Jesus' death in isolation from the entire work by which reconciliation between God and humanity is effected. The incarnation of the Son, his earthly ministry, his death and resurrection, and his ascension are together the one act of salvation by which God overcomes the forces of sin and death separating humanity from God. Perhaps the most important theme woven through-out the entire catechism is the triumph of God's suffering love. God's power is described in terms of God's love, "a love that is ready to suffer for our sakes, yet so strong that nothing will prevail against it" (question 8). The death of Jesus, thus, can be seen as the culmination of God's suffering love, which animates every aspect of his earthly ministry.

Nonetheless, Jesus' death on the cross has been singled out by the church as having special significance in the overall work of reconciliation. Look again at questions 43 and 44, noting the images used to explain the saving significance of Jesus' death.

Question 43. What do you affirm when you say that he was "crucified, dead and buried"?

That when our Lord passed through the door of real human death, he showed us that there is no sorrow he has not known, no grief he has not borne, and no price he was unwilling to pay in order to reconcile us to God.

Question 44. What do you affirm when you say that he "descended into hell"?

That our Lord took upon himself the full consequences of our sinfulness, even the agony of abandonment by God, in order that we might be spared.

The death of Christ on the cross is not the end of the story. With the women on Easter morning at the tomb we can proclaim "that our Lord could not be held by the power of death" (question 46). Christ's resurrection was hard for the disciples to believe. They did not believe the women until Jesus appeared to them. "In showing them his hands and his feet, the one who was crucified revealed himself to them as the Lord and Savior of the world" (question 46). Because Christ was raised from the dead, we know his birth, life, and suffering have importance beyond his own lifetime.

PROCLAIMING JESUS

We have a responsibility to share the good news of Christ with others. We are called to proclaim (Latin: *pro*, before + *clamare*, cry out). Our responsibility is to share with others the story of God's salvation, the events and meaning of the crucifixion, resurrection, and ascension. It is not our role to "save" others for Christ. God alone provides salvation. It is our responsibility to offer the message of salvation to others.

For God so loved the world that he gave his only Son, so that everyone who believes in him may not perish but may have eternal life. Indeed, God did not sent the Son into the world to condemn the world, but in order that the world might be saved through him. (John 3:16–17)

In our pluralistic world this is a challenge. The catechism (questions 50–52) offers helpful guidelines for how to address people of other religions. Scripture very clearly tells us "God has made salvation available to all human beings through Jesus Christ, crucified and risen" (question 51). Salvation is for all. We are called to proclaim the good news of how God is at work in our lives and in the world. We bear witness to God's love for the world in Jesus Christ. How has claiming Jesus as Lord and Savior changed your life? How is God at work in your life? We offer the message of the gospel, love those who believe differently, and pray that God will work in their lives, knowing that no one will be lost who can be saved.

Keeping a Journal

Reread the catechism questions and answers for this session. Choose one sentence or phrase to reflect on for the week. Here are some ideas:

- Christ aligned himself with all human beings who are oppressed, tortured, or otherwise shamefully treated by those with worldly power.
- There is no sorrow he has not known, no grief he has not borne, and no price he was unwilling to pay in order to reconcile us to God.
- Grace is more abundant—and sin more serious—than we suppose.
- The cross in all its severity reveals an abyss of sin swallowed up by the suffering of divine love.
- All the sinful failures that cause me shame will perish as through fire.
- No one will be lost who can be saved.
- I should always welcome and accept these others in a way that honors and reflects the Lord's welcome and acceptance of me.

See if you can memorize the sentence or phrase you choose, or at least remember the gist of it. Let this phrase stick with you through the week. Include it in your prayers, think about it while you are in the car, and remember it in the midst of a stressful situation. Look for connections between the phrase you selected and the world around you. Perhaps a conversation, a TV show, a current event, or a situation at home or at work will remind you of it. Record your thoughts and observations about this phrase and others in the journal space provided.

Who Is the Holy Spirit?

The *Study Catechism:* Questions 53–61

> ### Question 53. What is the third article of the Apostles' Creed?
>
> "I believe in the Holy Spirit, the holy catholic church, the communion of saints, the forgiveness of sins, the resurrection of the body, and the life everlasting. Amen."
>
> ### Question 54. What do you believe when you confess your faith in the Holy Spirit?
>
> Apart from the Holy Spirit, our Lord can neither be loved, nor known, nor served. The Holy Spirit is the personal bond by which Jesus Christ unites us to himself, the teacher who opens our hearts to Christ, and the comforter who leads us to repentance, empowering us to live in Christ's service. As the work of the one Holy Spirit, our love, knowledge, and service of Christ are all inseparably related.
>
> > *John 14:26* "But the Advocate, the Holy Spirit, whom the Father will send in my name, will teach you everything, and remind you of all that I have said to you."
> >
> > *1 Cor. 12:3* "No one can say 'Jesus is Lord' except by the Holy Spirit."
> >
> > *Rom. 5:5* "Hope does not disappoint us, because God's love has been poured into our hearts through the Holy Spirit that has been given to us."
> >
> > *1 Cor. 6:17, 19* "But anyone united to the Lord becomes one spirit with him. Or do you not know that your body is a temple of the Holy Spirit within you, which you have from God, and that you are not your own?"

1 Cor. 3:16 "Do you not know that you are God's temple and that God's Spirit dwells in you?"

John 4:24 "God is spirit, and those who worship him must worship in spirit and truth."

Question 55. How do we receive the Holy Spirit?

By receiving the Word of God. As the midwife of the new creation, the Spirit arrives with the Word, brings us to rebirth, and assures us of eternal life. The Spirit nurtures, corrects and strengthens us with the pure spiritual milk of the Word (1 Pet. 2:2).

Eph. 6:17 "Take the helmet of salvation, and the sword of the Spirit, which is the word of God."

John 14:16–17 "And I will ask the Father, and he will give you another Advocate, to be with you forever. This is the Spirit of truth, whom the world cannot receive, because it neither sees him nor knows him. You know him, because he abides with you, and he will be in you."

John 3:5–6 "Jesus answered, 'Very truly, I tell you, no one can enter the kingdom of God without being born of water and Spirit. What is born of the flesh is flesh, and what is born of the Spirit is spirit.'"

Luke 11:13 "If you then, who are evil, know how to give good gifts to your children, how much more will the heavenly Father give the Holy Spirit to those who ask him!"

1 Thess. 1:5 "Our message of the gospel came to you not in word only, but also in power and in the Holy Spirit and with full conviction; just as you know what kind of persons we proved to be among you for your sake."

John 16:8 "When he comes, he will prove the world wrong about sin and righteousness and judgment."

Rom. 8:15-16 "When we cry, 'Abba! Father!' it is that very Spirit bearing witness with our spirit that we are children of God."

1 Peter 2:2 "Like newborn infants, long for the pure, spiritual milk, so that by it you may grow into salvation."

Question 56. What do you mean when you speak of "the Word of God"?

"Jesus Christ as he is attested for us in Holy Scripture is the one Word of God whom we have to hear, and whom we have to trust and obey in life and in death" (Barmen Declaration, Article I).

> *John 1:1–5* "In the beginning was the Word, and the Word was with God, and the Word was God. He was in the beginning with God. All things came into being through him, and without him not one thing came into being. What has come into being in him was life, and the life was the light of all people. The light shines in the darkness, and the darkness did not overcome it."

> *John 1:14* "And the Word became flesh and lived among us, and we have seen his glory, the glory as of a father's only son, full of grace and truth."

Question 57. Isn't Holy Scripture also the Word of God?

Yes. Holy Scripture is also God's Word because of its content, its function, and its origin. Its central content is Jesus Christ, the living Word. Its basic function is to deepen our love, knowledge, and service of him as our Savior and Lord. And its ultimate origin is in the Holy Spirit, who spoke through the prophets and apostles, and who inspires us with eager desire for the truths that scripture contains.

> *2 Tim. 3:16* "All scripture is inspired by God and is useful for teaching, for reproof, for correction, and for training in righteousness."

> *John 5:39* "You search the scriptures because you think that in them you have eternal life; and it is they that testify on my behalf."

Question 58. Isn't preaching also the Word of God?

Yes. Preaching and other forms of Christian witness are also God's Word when they are faithful to the witness of Holy Scripture. By the power of the Spirit, preaching actually gives to us what it proclaims—the real presence of our Lord Jesus Christ. Faith comes by hearing God's Word in the form of faithful proclamation.

> *Mark 16:15* "And he said to them, 'Go into all the world and proclaim the good news to the whole creation.'"

> *2 Cor. 4:5* "For we do not proclaim ourselves; we proclaim Jesus Christ as Lord and ourselves as your slaves for Jesus' sake."

> *Rom. 1:15–16* "Hence my eagerness to proclaim the gospel to you also who are in Rome. For I am not ashamed of the gospel; it is the power of God for salvation to everyone who has faith, to the Jew first and also to the Greek."

Rom. 10:17 "So faith comes from what is heard, and what is heard comes through the word of Christ."

Question 59. Does the Holy Spirit ever speak apart from God's Word in its written and proclaimed forms?

Since the Spirit is not given to the church without the Word, true proclamation depends on scripture. Since the Word cannot be grasped without the Spirit, true interpretation depends on prayer. However, as the wind blows where it will, so may the Spirit speak or work in people's lives in unexpected or indirect ways, yet always according to the Word, never contradicting or diluting it.

John 3:8 "The wind blows where it chooses, and you hear the sound of it, but you do not know where it comes from or where it goes. So it is with everyone who is born of the Spirit."

Acts 8:29–31 "Then the Spirit said to Philip, 'Go over to this chariot and join it.' So Philip ran up to it and heard him reading the prophet Isaiah. He asked, 'Do you understand what you are reading?' He replied, 'How can I, unless someone guides me?' And he invited Philip to get in and sit beside him."

Eph. 6:18 "Pray in the Spirit at all times in every prayer and supplication. To that end keep alert and always persevere in supplication for all the saints."

2 Peter 1:20–21 "First of all you must understand this, that no prophecy of scripture is a matter of one's own interpretation, because no prophecy ever came by human will, but men and women moved by the Holy Spirit spoke from God."

Isa. 45:4 "I call you [Cyrus] by your name, I surname you, though you do not know me."

Num. 22:28 "Then the LORD opened the mouth of the donkey, and it said to Balaam, 'What have I done to you, that you have struck me these three times?'"

Question 60. Aren't people without faith sometimes wiser than those who have faith?

Yes. The important question for the church is not so much where an insight may come from as the norm by which to test it. Truth is where one finds it, whether inside or outside the church, and whether supporting or contradicting one's own most cherished opinions. Our faithful discernment of what is true, however, depends finally on God's Word as conveyed in Holy Scripture. The church is therefore reformed and always being reformed according to the Word of God.

> *Titus 1:9* "He must have a firm grasp of the word that is trustworthy in accordance with the teaching, so that he may be able both to preach with sound doctrine and to refute those who contradict it."

Question 61. Doesn't modern critical scholarship undermine your belief that Holy Scripture is a form of God's Word?

No. The methods of modern scholarship are a good servant but a bad master. They are neither to be accepted nor rejected uncritically. Properly used they help us rightly and richly interpret scripture; improperly used they can usurp the place of faith (or establish an alternative faith). Wise interpreters use these methods in the service of faithful witness and understanding. The methods of modern scholarship remain a useful tool, while Holy Scripture remains reliable in all essential matters of faith and practice.

> *Prov. 1:5–6* "Let the wise also hear and gain in learning, and the discerning acquire skill, to understand a proverb and a figure, the words of the wise and their riddles."

> *Prov. 10:14* "The wise lay up knowledge, but the babbling of a fool brings ruin near."

> *1 Cor. 1:20, 25* "Where is the one who is wise? Where is the scribe? Where is the debater of this age? Has not God made foolish the wisdom of the world? For God's foolishness is wiser than human wisdom, and God's weakness is stronger than human strength."

Reflections

With this session we begin the third and final section of the Apostles' Creed. We have talked about God and Jesus Christ. The third part of the Trinity is the Holy Spirit. It is the Holy Spirit that dwells with us today. Following the resurrection Jesus told the disciples that they would receive power from the Holy Spirit just before he ascended into heaven. On the day of Pentecost it is the Holy Spirit who descends upon the early believers, creating the church. With our study of the Holy Spirit we will study the church, the people within the church and the three great promises given to all believers.

THE HOLY SPIRIT

Who is the Holy Spirit? The Holy Spirit is the one who opens our hearts to Christ. The Holy Spirit leads us to repentance by helping us to examine our lives. The Holy Spirit empowers us to live in Christ's service. All that we do within the church and as a community of believers is because of the work of the Holy Spirit in our lives. It is through the Holy Spirit that we are united with Jesus Christ through the Word of God.

The Gospel of John tells us "In the beginning was the Word, and the Word was with God, and the Word was God." The Word of God became incarnate in the person of Jesus Christ. We know about Jesus Christ through the Holy Scriptures. The central content of scripture is Jesus Christ. The function of scripture is to deepen our love, knowledge, and service of Jesus Christ. The origin of scripture is the Holy Spirit who spoke through the prophets and apostles. As God's Word, Holy Scripture is reliable in all essential matters of faith and practice. Preaching is another form of the Word of God when the preaching is faithful to the witness of scripture.

Whenever we are trying to discern what the Word of God is for us today we must study the scriptures, hear the *word* proclaimed, seek God's guidance through prayer and then use the consistent message of the scriptures as a measuring rod. Through the centuries many scholars have done just this, and they provide us with many resources to aid us on our journey of faith. It is always important when reading the work of critical scholars to return to scripture and balance their insights with the Word of God. As members of the Reformed faith we have a motto: "We are reformed and always being reformed." This means we are always open to the scriptures read under the guidance of the Holy Spirit to blow fresh insights into our understanding and cause us to think afresh about God's Word for us.

The Holy Spirit is at work in our world today. Where have you seen the Spirit at work? For some, the experience of the Holy Spirit is as powerful as the events of the day of Pentecost recorded in Acts 2. For others, it might be as simple as the sharing of the meaning of scripture, as Philip did with the Ethiopian eunuch. The Holy Spirit is alive and well in our world today. Look around you for signs of God's wind blowing anew.

Keeping a Journal

1. Reread the catechism questions and answers for this session. Choose one sentence or phrase to reflect on for the week. Here are some ideas:

- The Holy Spirit is the personal bond by which Jesus Christ unites us to himself, the teacher who opens our hearts to Christ, and the comforter who leads us to repentance, empowering us to live in Christ's service.

- As the midwife of the new creation, the Spirit arrives with the Word, brings us to rebirth, and assures us of eternal life.

- Faith comes by hearing God's Word in the form of faithful proclamation.

- Truth is where one finds it, whether inside or outside the church, and whether supporting or contradicting one's own most cherished opinions.

See if you can memorize the sentence or phrase you choose, or at least remember the gist of it. Let this phrase stick with you through the week. Include it in your prayers, think about it while you are in the car, and remember it in the midst of a stressful situation. Look for connections between the phrase you selected and the world around you. Perhaps a conversation, a TV show, a current event, or a situation at home or at work will remind you of it. Record your thoughts and observations about this phrase and others in the journal space provided.

2. Reflect upon your faith journey. When have you experienced the Holy Spirit at work? Was it a powerful event or a still small voice? Do you feel the Spirit at work in your life right now? How might you gain more sense of the Spirit in your life? Pray "Spirit of the living God, fall afresh on me," and be silent for at least five minutes to give the Spirit time to speak to you.

The Church and the Sacraments

The *Study Catechism:* Questions 62–79

> ### Question 62. What do you affirm when you speak of "the holy catholic church"?
>
> The church is the company of all faithful people who have given their lives to Jesus Christ, as he has given and gives himself to them. Since Christ cannot be separated from his people, the church is holy because he is holy, and universal (or "catholic") in significance because he is universal in significance. Despite all its remaining imperfections here and now, the church is called to become ever more holy and catholic, for that is what it already is in Christ.
>
> *Gal. 2:20* "And the life I now live in the flesh I live by faith in the Son of God, who loved me and gave himself for me."
>
> *1 Cor. 1:2* "To the church of God that is in Corinth, to those who are sanctified in Christ Jesus, called to be saints, together with all those who in every place call on the name of our Lord Jesus Christ, both their Lord and ours . . ."
>
> *Lev. 11:44* "For I am the LORD your God; sanctify yourselves therefore, and be holy, for I am holy."
>
> *1 Peter 1:15–16* "Instead, as he who called you is holy, be holy yourselves in all your conduct; for it is written, 'You shall be holy, for I am holy.'"
>
> *Rev. 5:9* "They sing a new song: 'You are worthy to take the scroll and to open its seals, for you were slaughtered and by your blood you ransomed for God saints from every tribe and language and people and nation.'"

Question 63. What is the mission of the church?

The mission of the church is to bear witness to God's love for the world in Jesus Christ.

Acts 1:8 "But you will receive power when the Holy Spirit has come upon you; and you will be my witnesses in Jerusalem, in all Judea and Samaria, and to the ends of the earth."

John 15:26–27 "When the Advocate comes, whom I will send to you from the Father, the Spirit of truth who comes from the Father, he will testify on my behalf. You also are to testify because you have been with me from the beginning."

Eph. 3:8–10 "Although I am the very least of all the saints, this grace was given to me to bring to the Gentiles the news of the boundless riches of Christ, and to make everyone see what is the plan of the mystery hidden for ages in God who created all things; so that through the church the wisdom of God in its rich variety might now be made known to the rulers and authorities in the heavenly places."

Question 64. What forms does this mission take?

The forms are as various as the forms of God's love, yet the center is always Jesus Christ. The church is faithful to its mission when it extends mercy and forgiveness to the needy in ways that point finally to him. For in the end it is always by Christ's mercy that the needs of the needy are met.

Luke 10:36 "'Which of these three, do you think, was a neighbor to the man who fell into the hands of the robbers?' He said, 'The one who showed him mercy.' Jesus said to him, 'Go and do likewise.'"

Eph. 4:32 "Be kind to one another, tenderhearted, forgiving one another, as God in Christ has forgiven you."

Deut. 15:11 "Since there will never cease to be some in need on the earth, I therefore command you, 'Open your hand to the poor and needy neighbor in your land.'"

Acts 4:34 "There was not a needy person among them, for as many as owned lands or houses sold them and brought the proceeds of what was sold."

Question 65. Who are the needy?

The hungry need bread, the homeless need a roof, the oppressed need justice, and the lonely need fellowship. At the same time—on another and deeper level—the hopeless need hope, sinners need forgiveness, and the world needs the gospel. On this level no one is excluded, and all the needy are one. Our mission as the church is to bring hope to a desperate world by declaring God's undying love—as one beggar tells another where to find bread.

> *Ps. 10:12*   "Rise up, O Lord; O God, lift up your hand; do not forget the oppressed."

> *Matt. 25:37–40*   "Then the righteous will answer him, 'Lord, when was it that we saw you hungry and gave you food, or thirsty and gave you something to drink? And when was it that we saw you a stranger and welcomed you, or naked and gave you clothing? And when was it that we saw you sick or in prison and visited you?' And the king will answer them, 'Truly I tell you, just as you did it to one of the least of these who are members of my family, you did it to me.'"

> *Jer. 9:23*   "Thus says the LORD: Do not let the wise boast in their wisdom, do not let the mighty boast in their might, do not let the wealthy boast in their wealth."

> *1 Cor. 9:16*   "Woe to me if I do not proclaim the gospel!"

> *Eph. 6:19*   "Pray also for me, so that when I speak, a message may be given to me to make known with boldness the mystery of the gospel."

Question 66. *What do you affirm when you speak of "the communion of saints"?*

All those who live in union with Christ, whether on earth or with God in heaven, are "saints." Our communion with Christ makes us members one of another. As by his death he removed our separation from God, so by his Spirit he removes all that divides us from each other. Breaking down every wall of hostility, he makes us, who are many, one body in himself. The ties that bind us in Christ are deeper than any other human relationship.

> *Eph. 2:19–20*   "You are no longer strangers and aliens, but you are citizens with the saints and also members of the household of God, built upon the foundation of the apostles and prophets, with Christ Jesus himself as the cornerstone."

> *Rom. 12:5*   "So we, who are many, are one body in Christ, and individually we are members one of another."

> *Eph. 2:14*   "For he is our peace; in his flesh he has made both groups into one and has broken down the dividing wall, that is, the hostility between us."

1 Cor. 12:27 "Now you are the body of Christ and individually members of it."

Gal. 3:28 "There is no longer Jew or Greek, there is no longer slave or free, there is no longer male and female; for all of you are one in Christ Jesus."

Eph. 4:4 "There is one body and one Spirit, just as you were called to the one hope of your calling."

1 Cor. 12:4–7, 12–13 "Now there are varieties of gifts, but the same Spirit; and there are varieties of services, but the same Lord; and there are varieties of activities, but it is the same God who activates all of them in everyone. To each is given the manifestation of the Spirit for the common good. For just as the body is one and has many members, and all the members of the body, though many, are one body, so it is with Christ. For in the one Spirit we were all baptized into one body—Jews or Greeks, slaves or free—and we were all made to drink of one Spirit."

Question 67. How do you enter into communion with Christ and so with one another?

By the power of the Holy Spirit as it works through Word and sacrament. Because the Spirit uses them for our salvation, Word and sacrament are called "means of grace." The Scriptures acknowledge two sacraments as instituted by our Lord Jesus Christ—baptism and the Lord's Supper.

1 Cor. 10:17 "Because there is one bread, we who are many are one body, for we all partake of the one bread."

1 Cor. 12:13 "For in the one Spirit we were all baptized into one body—Jews or Greeks, slaves or free—and we were all made to drink of one Spirit."

Col. 3:16 "Let the word of Christ dwell in you richly."

Question 68. What is a sacrament?

A sacrament is a special act of Christian worship, instituted by Christ, which uses a visible sign to proclaim the promise of the gospel for the forgiveness of sins and eternal life. The sacramental sign seals this promise to believers by grace and brings to them what is promised. In baptism the sign is that of water; in the Lord's Supper, that of bread and wine.

Mark 1:9–11 "In those days Jesus came from Nazareth of Galilee and was baptized by John in the Jordan. And just as he was coming up out of the water, he saw the heavens torn apart and the Spirit descending like a dove on him. And a voice came from heaven, "You are my Son, the Beloved; with you I am well pleased.'"

Mark 14:22–25 "While they were eating, he took a loaf of bread, and after blessing it he broke it, gave it to them, and said, 'Take; this is my body.' Then he took a cup, and after giving thanks he gave it to them, and all of them drank from it. He said to them, 'This is my blood of the covenant, which is poured out for many. Truly I tell you, I will never again drink of the fruit of the vine until that day when I drink it new in the kingdom of God.'"

Question 69. How do you understand the relationship between the word of promise and the sacramental sign?

Take away the word of promise, and the water is merely water, or the bread and wine, merely bread and wine. But add water, or bread and wine, to the word of promise, and it becomes a visible word. In this form it does what by grace the word always does: it brings the salvation it promises, and conveys to faith the real presence of our Lord Jesus Christ. The sacraments are visible words which uniquely assure and confirm that no matter how greatly I may have sinned, Christ died also for me, and comes to live in me and with me.

Luke 24:30–31 "When he was at the table with them, he took bread, blessed and broke it, and gave it to them. Then their eyes were opened, and they recognized him; and he vanished from their sight."

1 Cor. 10:16 "The cup of blessing that we bless, is it not a sharing in the blood of Christ? The bread that we break, is it not a sharing in the body of Christ?"

Matt. 28:20 "[Teach] them to obey everything that I have commanded you. And remember, I am with you always, to the end of the age."

Col. 1:27 "To them God chose to make known how great among the Gentiles are the riches of the glory of this mystery, which is Christ in you, the hope of glory."

Question 70. What is the main difference between baptism and the Lord's Supper?

While I receive baptism only once, I receive the Lord's Supper again and again. Being unrepeatable, baptism indicates not only that Christ died for our sins once and for all, but that by grace we are also united with him once and for all through faith.

Being repeatable, the Lord's Supper indicates that as we turn unfilled to him again and again, our Lord continually meets us in the power of the Holy Spirit to renew and deepen our faith.

Acts 2:41 "So those who welcomed his message were baptized, and that day about three thousand persons were added."

John 6:33 "For the bread of God is that which comes down from heaven and gives life to the world."

John 6:51 "I am the living bread that came down from heaven. Whoever eats of this bread will live forever; and the bread that I will give for the life of the world is my flesh."

John 6:56 "Those who eat my flesh and drink my blood abide in me, and I in them."

1 Cor. 11:26 "For as often as you eat this bread and drink the cup, you proclaim the Lord's death until he comes."

Question 71. What is baptism?

Baptism is the sign and seal through which we are joined to Christ.

Rom. 6:3–4 "Do you not know that all of us who have been baptized into Christ Jesus were baptized into his death? Therefore we have been buried with him by baptism into death, so that, just as Christ was raised from the dead by the glory of the Father, so we too might walk in newness of life."

Gal. 3:27 "As many of you as were baptized into Christ have clothed yourselves with Christ."

Rom. 4:11 "[Abraham] received the sign of circumcision as a seal of the righteousness that he had by faith."

Question 72. What does it mean to be baptized?

My baptism means that I am joined to Jesus Christ forever. I am baptized into his death and resurrection, along with all who have received him by faith. As I am baptized with water, he baptizes me with his Spirit, washing away all my sins and freeing me from their control. My baptism is a sign that one day I will rise with him in glory, and may walk with him even now in newness of life.

Col. 2:12 "When you were buried with him in baptism, you were also raised with him through faith in the power of God, who raised him from the dead."

Mark 1:8 "I have baptized you with water; but he will baptize you with the Holy Spirit."

1 Cor. 6:11 "You were washed, you were sanctified, you were justi-fied in the name of the Lord Jesus Christ and in the Spirit of our God."

Eph. 4:4–6 "There is one body and one Spirit, just as you were called to the one hope of your calling, one Lord, one faith, one bap-tism, one God and Father of all, who is above all and through all and in all."

Question 73. Are infants also to be baptized?

Yes. Along with their believing parents, they are included in the great hope of the gospel and belong to the people of God. Forgiveness and faith are both promised to them as gifts through Christ's covenant with his people. These children are therefore to be received into the community by baptism, nur-tured in the Word of God, and confirmed at an appropriate time by their own profession of faith.

Gen. 17:7 "I will establish my covenant between me and you, and your offspring after you throughout their generations, for an ever-lasting covenant, to be God to you and to your offspring after you."

Acts 2:38–39 "Peter said to them, 'Repent, and be baptized every one of you in the name of Jesus Christ so that your sins may be for-given; and you will receive the gift of the Holy Spirit. For the promise is for you, for your children, and for all who are far away, everyone whom the Lord our God calls to him.'"

Acts 16:15 "When she and her household were baptized, she urged us, saying, 'If you have judged me to be faithful to the Lord, come and stay at my home.' And she prevailed upon us."

Acts 16:33 "At the same hour of the night he took them and washed their wounds; then he and his entire family were baptized without delay."

Acts 18:8 "Crispus, the official of the synagogue, became a be-liever in the Lord, together with all his household; and many of the Corinthians who heard Paul became believers and were baptized."

Question 74. Should infants be baptized if their parents or guardians have no relation to the church?

No. It would be irresponsible to baptize an infant without at least one Christian parent or guardian who promises to nurture the infant in the life of the community and to instruct it in the Christian faith.

Eph. 6:4 "Bring [your children] up in the discipline and instruction of the Lord."

2 Tim. 1:5 "I am reminded of your sincere faith, a faith that lived first in your grandmother Lois and your mother Eunice and now, I am sure, lives in you."

1 Cor. 7:14 "For the unbelieving husband is made holy through his wife, and the unbelieving wife is made holy through her husband. Otherwise, your children would be unclean, but as it is, they are holy."

Question 75. In what name are you baptized?

In the name of the Trinity. After he was raised from the dead, our Lord appeared to his disciples and said to them, "Go and make disciples of all nations, baptizing them in the name of the Father and of the Son and of the Holy Spirit" (Matt. 28:19).

Matt. 28:16–20 "Now the eleven disciples went to Galilee, to the mountain to which Jesus had directed them. When they saw him, they worshipped him; but some doubted. And Jesus came and said to them, 'All authority in heaven and on earth has been given to me. Go therefore and make disciples of all nations, baptizing them in the name of the Father and of the Son and of the Holy Spirit, and teaching them to obey everything that I have commanded you. And remember, I am with you always, to the end of the age.'"

Matt. 3:16–17 "And when Jesus had been baptized, just as he came up from the water, suddenly the heavens were opened to him and he saw the Spirit of God descending like a dove and alighting on him. And a voice from heaven said, 'This is my Son, the Beloved, with whom I am well pleased.'"

1 Peter 1:1–2 "To the exiles . . . who have been chosen and destined by God the Father and sanctified by the Spirit to be obedient to Jesus Christ and to be sprinkled with his blood: May grace and peace be yours in abundance."

1 Cor. 12:4–6 "Now there are varieties of gifts, but the same Spirit; and there are varieties of services, but the same Lord; and there are varieties of activities, but it is the same God who activates all of them in everyone."

Question 76. What is the meaning of this name?

It is the name of the Holy Trinity. The Father is God, the Son is God, and the Holy Spirit is God. And yet they are not three gods, but one God in three persons. We worship God in this mystery.

2 Cor. 13:13 "The grace of the Lord Jesus Christ, the love of God, and the communion of the Holy Spirit be with all of you."

John 1:1–4 "In the beginning was the Word, and the Word was with God, and the Word was God. He was in the beginning with God. All things came into being through him, and without him not one thing came into being. What has come into being in him was life, and the life was the light of all people."

Rom. 8:11 "If the Spirit of him who raised Jesus from the dead dwells in you, he who raised Christ from the dead will give life to your mortal bodies also through his Spirit that dwells in you."

John 16:13–15 "When the Spirit of truth comes, he will guide you into all the truth. . . . He will glorify me, because he will take what is mine and declare it to you. All that the Father has is mine. For this reason I said that he will take what is mine and declare it to you."

Question 77. What is the Lord's Supper?

The Lord's Supper is the sign and seal by which our communion with Christ is renewed.

1 Cor. 10:16 "The cup of blessing that we bless, is it not a sharing in the blood of Christ? The bread that we break, is it not a sharing in the body of Christ?"

Question 78. What does it mean to share in the Lord's Supper?

When we celebrate the Lord's Supper, the Lord Jesus Christ is truly present, pouring out his Spirit upon us. By his Spirit, the bread that we break and the cup that we bless share in our Lord's own body and blood. Through them he once offered our life to God; through them he now offers his life to us. As I receive the bread and the cup, remembering that Christ died even for me, I feed on him in my heart by faith with thanksgiving, and enter his risen life, so that his life becomes mine, and my life becomes his, to all eternity.

1 Cor. 11:23–26 "For I received from the Lord what I also handed on to you, that the Lord Jesus on the night when he was betrayed took a loaf of bread, and when he had given thanks, he broke it and said, 'This is my body that is for you. Do this in remembrance of me.' In the same way he took the cup also, after supper, saying, 'This cup is the new covenant in my blood. Do this, as often as you drink it, in remembrance of me.' For as often as you eat this bread and drink the cup, you proclaim the Lord's death until he comes."

> *Mark 14:22–25* "While they were eating, he took a loaf of bread, and after blessing it he broke it, gave it to them, and said, 'Take; this is my body.' Then he took a cup, and after giving thanks he gave it to them, and all of them drank from it. He said to them, 'This is my blood of the covenant, which is poured out for many. Truly I tell you, I will never again drink of the fruit of the vine until that day when I drink it new in the kingdom of God.'"

Question 79. Who may receive the Lord's Supper?

All baptized Christians who rejoice in so great a gift, who confess their sins, and who draw near with faith intending to lead a new life, may receive the Lord's Supper. This includes baptized children who have expressed a desire to participate and who have been instructed in the meaning of the sacrament in a way they can understand.

> *Luke 13:29* "Then people will come from east and west, from north and south, and will eat in the kingdom of God."

> *1 Cor. 11:28* "Examine yourselves, and only then eat of the bread and drink of the cup."

> *Phil. 4:4* "Rejoice in the Lord always; again I will say, Rejoice."

Reflections

The Holy Spirit is alive and well in the world today! We as Christians need to be aware of the places where the Spirit is at work. There are two major ways for Christians to respond to the work of the Holy Spirit. The first is by involvement in the church and its mission. The second is through worship and the sacraments.

THE CHURCH AND ITS MISSION

Following the life, death, resurrection, and ascension of Jesus, the disciples gathered together to figure out what to do next. On the day of Pentecost, Peter boldly proclaimed Jesus as Lord and Christ. In response, three thousand people were added to the followers of Christ, and the movement known as the church was begun. Christians live in relationship with Jesus Christ and in relationship with others who profess faith in Christ. We cannot be "lone ranger" Christians. When we speak of the "holy catholic church" we affirm that we are connected with Christians in every time and place because of our relationship with Christ.

The catechism explains that the mission of the church "is to bear witness to God's love for the world in Jesus Christ." It is the responsibility of the church to proclaim Jesus Christ as Lord and Savior. The church testifies in word and in deed to what God has done for the world in Jesus Christ. The Book of Order of the Presbyterian Church (U.S.A.) states this another way: "The great ends of the church are the proclamation of the gospel for the salvation of humankind; the shelter, nurture, and spiritual fellowship of the children of God; the maintenance of divine worship; the preservation of the truth; the promotion of social righteousness; and the exhibition of the Kingdom of Heaven to the world." Each individual congregation decides the form its mission will take, but the center of this mission is always Jesus Christ. Jesus models a variety of ways for Christians to care for others. How are you as a Christian involved in the mission of the church? In what ways do you reach out to others with the love of Christ? Sharing God's love is not an option for Christians. It is a responsibility and a calling.

WORSHIP AND SACRAMENTS

As Christians, we respond to the work of the Holy Spirit when we worship. The act of Christian worship is an opportunity to visibly proclaim Jesus Christ as Lord and Savior and to center our lives on God. We worship to say thank you to God for the many blessings we have and for the gift of Jesus Christ. As Presbyterians, we center ourselves on the Word of God and the sacraments. It is through the proclamation of the Word (preaching) and the faithful enactment of the two sacraments instituted by Jesus (Baptism and the Lord's Supper) that we affirm the promises of scripture. The sacraments offer a sign and a seal of what God has already done for us in the life, death, and resurrection of Jesus Christ.

The sacrament of Baptism uses water as a sign and seal of the promises of God. In baptism we are united with Jesus Christ once and for all through faith. Baptism is only received once. The promises of baptism are for believers and their children. As faithful Christians we offer our children for the sacrament of Baptism and promise to bring them up in the nurture and admonition of the Lord. We are baptized in the name of the Father, Son and Holy Spirit—the Trinity.

The sacrament of the Lord's Supper was instituted by Christ during the last supper he shared with his disciples. The Lord's Supper is a repeatable sacrament that reminds us each time we partake of the sacrifice Christ made for us on the cross and the promise that the Lord is always with us. In the Lord's Supper the visible signs are the bread and the wine or grape juice. Through Christ's Spirit "the bread that we break and the cup that we bless share in our Lord's own body and blood" (question 78). When we partake of the bread and the cup we remember the sacrifice Jesus made for us and enter into Christ's risen life by faith. All baptized Christians are invited to participate in the Lord's Supper.

Jesus Christ came to live among us as a gift for each of us. Our proper response to that gift is to worship God, proclaiming Jesus Christ as Lord and Savior and celebrating our relationship with God. When we gather in worship we witness to the resurrection of Christ. Our worship is also a proclamation of the many ways the Spirit is at work today. We are nourished by the preaching of God's Word and by the sacraments and sent out into the world to witness to God's love in Jesus Christ.

Keeping a Journal

1. Reread the catechism questions and answers for this session. Choose one sentence or phrase to reflect on for the week. Here are some ideas:

   - Despite all its remaining imperfections here and now, the church is called to become ever more holy and catholic, for that is what it already is in Christ.

   - The mission of the church is to bear witness to God's love for the world in Jesus Christ.

   - Our mission as the church is to bring hope to a desperate world by declaring God's undying love—as one beggar tells another where to find bread.

   - The sacramental sign seals this promise to believers by grace and brings to them what is promised.

   - No matter how greatly I may have sinned, Christ died also for me, and comes to live in me and with me.

   - As I receive the bread and the cup, remembering that Christ died even for me, I feed on him in my heart by faith with thanksgiving and enter his risen life, so that his life becomes mine and my life becomes his, to all eternity.

   See if you can memorize the sentence or phrase you choose, or at least remember the gist of it. Let this phrase stick with you through the week. Include it in your prayers, think about it while you are in the car, and remember it in the midst of a stressful situation. Look for connections between the phrase you selected and the world around you. Perhaps a conversation, a TV show, a current event, or a situation at home or at work will remind you of it. Record your thoughts and observations about this phrase and others in the journal space provided.

2. Reflect on the last time you partook of the Lord's Supper or witnessed a baptism. What did you experience? What roles have the sacraments played in your life? How important is worship in your life? How comfortable are you with sharing the gospel with those in need? In which of these areas do you need to ask for God's strength, guidance, and courage as you grow? Offer these areas up to God in prayer.

Gifts of God: Forgiveness, Resurrection, and Life Everlasting

The *Study Catechism*: Questions 80–88

Question 80. What do you mean when you speak of "the forgiveness of sins"?

That because of Jesus Christ, God no longer holds my sins against me. Christ alone is my righteousness and my life; Christ is my only hope. Grace alone, not my merits, is the basis on which God has forgiven me in him. Faith alone, not my works, is the means by which I receive Christ into my heart, and with him the forgiveness that makes me whole. Christ alone, grace alone, and faith alone bring the forgiveness I receive through the gospel.

1 Cor. 1:30 "Christ Jesus became for us wisdom from God, and righteousness and sanctification and redemption."

1 Tim. 1:1 "Paul, an apostle by the command of God our Savior and of Christ Jesus our hope."

Rom. 11:6 "But if it is by grace, it is no longer on the basis of works, otherwise grace would no longer be grace."

Eph. 2:8 "For by grace you have been saved through faith, and this is not your own doing; it is the gift of God."

Rom. 5:15 "But the free gift is not like the trespass. For if the many died through the one man's trespass, much more surely have the grace of God and the free gift in the grace of the one man, Jesus Christ, abounded for the many."

Rom. 4:16 "For this reason it depends on faith, in order that the promise may rest on grace and be guaranteed to all his descendants, not only to the adherents of the law but also to those who share the faith of Abraham."

Rom. 3:28 "For we hold that a person is justified by faith apart from works prescribed by the law."

Question 81. Does forgiveness mean that God condones sin?

No. God does not cease to be God. Although God is merciful, God does not condone what God forgives. In the death and resurrection of Christ, God judges what God abhors—everything hostile to love—by abolishing it at the very roots. In this judgment the unexpected occurs: good is brought out of evil, hope out of hopelessness, and life out of death. God spares sinners and turns them from enemies into friends. The uncompromising judgment of God is revealed in the suffering love of the cross.

Hab. 1:13 "Your eyes are too pure to behold evil, and you cannot look on wrongdoing; why do you look on the treacherous, and are silent when the wicked swallow those more righteous than they?"

Isa. 59:15 "The LORD saw it, and it displeased him that there was no justice."

Heb. 9:22 "Indeed, under the law almost everything is purified with blood, and without the shedding of blood there is no forgiveness of sins."

Rom. 5:8–10 "But God proves his love for us in that while we still were sinners Christ died for us. Much more surely then, now that we have been justified by his blood, will we be saved through him from the wrath of God. For if while we were enemies, we were reconciled to God through the death of his Son, much more surely, having been reconciled, will we be saved by his life."

1 Chron. 16:33 "Then shall the trees of the forest sing for joy before the LORD, for he comes to judge the earth."

Question 82. Does your forgiveness of those who have harmed you depend on their repentance?

No. I am to forgive as I have been forgiven. The gospel is the astonishing good news that while we were yet sinners Christ died for us. Just as God's forgiveness of me is unconditional, and so precedes my confession of sin and repentance, so my forgiveness of those who have harmed me does not depend on their confessing and repenting of their sin. However, when I forgive the person who has done me harm, giving up any resentment or desire to retaliate, I do not condone the harm that was done or excuse the evil of the sin.

Col. 3:13 "Just as the Lord has forgiven you, so you also must forgive."

Mark 11:25 "Whenever you stand praying, forgive, if you have anything against anyone; so that your Father in heaven may also forgive you your trespasses."

Col. 2:13 "When you were dead in trespasses and the uncircumcision of your flesh, God made you alive together with him, when he forgave us all our trespasses."

Matt. 18:21–22 "Then Peter came and said to him, 'Lord, if another member of the church sins against me, how often should I forgive? As many as seven times?' Jesus said to him, 'Not seven times, but, I tell you, seventy-seven times.'"

Heb. 12:14 "Pursue peace with everyone, and the holiness without which no one will see the Lord."

Question 83. How can you forgive those who have really hurt you?

I cannot love my enemies, I cannot pray for those who persecute me, I cannot even be ready to forgive those who have really hurt me, without the grace that comes from above. I cannot be conformed to the image of God's Son, apart from the power of God's Word and Spirit. Yet I am promised that I can do all things through Christ who strengthens me.

Luke 6:27–28 "But I say to you that listen, Love your enemies, do good to those who hate you, bless those who curse you, pray for those who abuse you."

James 1:17 "Every generous act of giving, with every perfect gift, is from above, coming down from the Father of lights, with whom there is no variation or shadow due to change."

Rom. 8:29 "For those whom he foreknew he also predestined to be conformed to the image of his Son, in order that he might be the firstborn within a large family."

Phil. 4:13 "I can do all things through him who strengthens me."

Question 84. What do you mean when you speak of "the resurrection of the body"?

Because Christ lives, we will live also. The resurrection of the body celebrates our eternal value to God as living persons, each one with a unique and distinctive identity. Indeed, the living

Savior who goes before us was once heard, seen, and touched in person, after the discovery of his empty tomb. The resurrection of the body means hope for the whole person, because it is in the unity of body and soul, not in soul alone, that I belong in life and in death to my faithful Savior Jesus Christ.

> *John 14:19* "In a little while the world will no longer see me, but you will see me; because I live, you also will live."

> *John 11:25* "Jesus said to her, 'I am the resurrection and the life. Those who believe in me, even though they die, will live.'"

> *Rom. 6:5* "For if we have been united with him in a death like his, we will certainly be united with him in a resurrection like his."

> *1 Cor. 15:21* "For since death came through a human being, the resurrection of the dead has also come through a human being."

> *1 Cor. 15:42* "So it is with the resurrection of the dead. What is sown is perishable, what is raised is imperishable."

> *Col. 1:18* "He is the head of the body, the church; he is the beginning, the firstborn from the dead."

Question 85. What is the nature of resurrection hope?

Resurrection hope is a hope for the transformation of this world, not a hope for escape from it. It is the hope that evil in all its forms will be utterly eradicated, that past history will be redeemed, and that all the things that ever were will be made new. It is the hope of a new creation, a new heaven, and a new earth, in which God is really honored as God, human beings are truly loving, and peace and justice reign on earth.

> *Isa. 11:6* "The wolf shall live with the lamb, the leopard shall lie down with the kid, the calf and the lion and the fatling together, and a little child shall lead them."

> *Rev. 21:1* "Then I saw a new heaven and a new earth; for the first heaven and the first earth had passed away, and the sea was no more."

> *Isa. 65:17* "For I am about to create new heavens and a new earth; the former things shall not be remembered or come to mind."

> *2 Peter 3:13* "But, in accordance with his promise, we wait for new heavens and a new earth, where righteousness is at home."

> *2 Cor. 5:17* "So if anyone is in Christ, there is a new creation: everything old has passed away; see, everything has become new!"

Question 86. Does resurrection hope mean that we don't have to take action to relieve the suffering of this world?

No. When the great hope is truly alive, small hopes arise even now for alleviating the sufferings of the present time. Reconciliation—with God, with one another, and with oneself—is the great hope God has given to the world. While we commit to God the needs of the whole world in our prayers, we also know that we are commissioned to be instruments of God's peace. When hostility, injustice and suffering are overcome here and now, we anticipate the end of all things—the life that God brings out of death, which is the meaning of resurrection hope.

> *Ps. 27:13* "I believe that I shall see the goodness of the LORD in the land of the living."

> *Ps. 33:20–22* "Our soul waits for the LORD; he is our help and shield. Our heart is glad in him, because we trust in his holy name. Let your steadfast love, O LORD, be upon us, even as we hope in you."

> *Rom. 14:19* "Let us then pursue what makes for peace and for mutual upbuilding."

> *Deut. 30:19* "I call heaven and earth to witness against you today that I have set before you life and death, blessings and curses. Choose life so that you and your descendants may live."

> *Luke 1:78* "By the tender mercy of our God, the dawn from on high will break upon us."

Question 87. What do you affirm when you speak of "the life everlasting"?

That God does not will to be God without us, but instead grants to us creatures—fallen and mortal as we are—eternal life. Communion with Jesus Christ is eternal life itself. In him we were chosen before the foundation of the world. By him the eternal covenant with Israel was taken up, embodied, and fulfilled. To him we are joined by the Holy Spirit through faith and adopted as children, the sons and daughters of God. Through him we are raised from death to new life. For him we shall live to all eternity.

> *John 3:16* "For God so loved the world that he gave his only Son, so that everyone who believes in him may not perish but may have eternal life."

John 6:54 "Those who eat my flesh and drink my blood have eternal life, and I will raise them up on the last day."

John 17:3 "And this is eternal life, that they may know you, the only true God, and Jesus Christ whom you have sent."

Rom. 6:22 "But now that you have been freed from sin and enslaved to God, the advantage you get is sanctification. The end is eternal life."

Rom. 6:23 "For the wages of sin is death, but the free gift of God is eternal life in Christ Jesus our Lord."

1 John 2:25 "And this is what he has promised us, eternal life."

Matt. 25:34 "Then the king will say to those at his right hand, 'Come, you that are blessed by my Father, inherit the kingdom prepared for you from the foundation of the world.'"

Question 88. Won't heaven be a boring place?

No. Heaven is our true home, a world of love. There the Spirit shall be poured out into every heart in perfect love. There the Father and the Son are united in the loving bond of the Spirit. There we shall be united with them and one another. There we shall at last see face to face what we now only glimpse as through a distant mirror. Our deepest, truest delights in this life are only a dim foreshadowing of the delights that await us in heaven. "You show me the path of life. In your presence there is fullness of joy; in your right hand are pleasures forevermore" (Ps. 16:11).

John 14:2–3 "In my Father's house there are many dwelling places. If it were not so, would I have told you that I go to prepare a place for you? And if I go and prepare a place for you, I will come again and will take you to myself, so that where I am, there you may be also."

Matt. 6:20 "But store up for yourselves treasures in heaven, where neither moth nor rust consumes and where thieves do not break in and steal."

Matt. 8:11 "I tell you, many will come from east and west and will eat with Abraham and Isaac and Jacob in the kingdom of heaven."

Col. 1:4–5 "For we have heard of your faith in Christ Jesus and of the love that you have for all the saints, because of the hope laid up for you in heaven. You have heard of this hope before in the word of the truth, the gospel."

> *1 Cor. 13:12* "For now we see in a mirror, dimly, but then we will see face to face. Now I know only in part; then I will know fully, even as I have been fully known."

Reflections

The Apostles' Creed ends with three powerful promises of hope that are ours from Jesus Christ through the Holy Spirit. On these three promises rests the essence of what faith in Jesus Christ means. They are the promises that we claim and look toward as we seek to live as faithful disciples.

FORGIVENESS OF SINS

The first of these promises is the forgiveness of sins. The catechism states the means of this very simply: "God no longer holds my sins against me" (question 80). We know that we are all sinners and fall short of the glory of God, but because Christ died for us (God's gift of grace), we know that we are forgiven. We cannot earn this promise of forgiveness. It is a gift, freely given. This gift does not give us permission to sin, nor does it excuse or condone our sin.

Learning how to forgive those who hurt us as Christ has forgiven us is one of the biggest challenges of our lives. Forgiveness does not come easily. However, by God's grace we are able to forgive as we have been forgiven. With Christ in our lives we can move toward forgiveness in a new way. God forgives us. Can we forgive others? Are there people in your life that you have found hard to forgive? Examine what it is about the relationship that makes forgiveness difficult. Offer this relationship to God in prayer.

RESURRECTION OF THE BODY

The second promise is the resurrection of the body. God created us as human beings. God sent Jesus Christ to earth where he died but was raised to a new life. This is the promise of the resurrection of the body for each of us. We are valuable to God and God remains in relationship with us even after death. The promise of the resurrection is a promise that in life and in death we belong to God. Scripture promises a new heaven and a new earth where everything will be different. All the pain and hardships of life on earth will be transformed by the love of God in Christ. Living as believers in the resurrection hope means we do not fear death. We see it as part of our journey. It also means we work while we are on earth to bring peace and joy to all. The resurrection hope means we live our life on earth not in fear but in gratitude for the future life God promises us. Death is not the end of the story.

LIFE EVERLASTING

The final hope is "life everlasting." We are promised that with the resurrection hope comes the promise of life with God always. We will never be separated from God. We are promised eternal life with God. No one knows exactly what heaven is like, but we do know that to be in heaven is to be with God and to experience life as we have never known it before. "Heaven is our true home, a world of love" (question 88). The Holy Spirit will pour out love so that there is no animosity, no hurt, no pain. We will be full of joy in heaven.

This lesson concludes the study of the Apostles' Creed. Through the words of the Apostles' Creed, Christians around the world proclaim what it is we believe about God, Jesus Christ, and the Holy Spirit. Each time you repeat the Apostles' Creed in the future, proclaim these words with a new commitment.

Keeping a Journal

1. Reread the catechism questions and answers for this session. Choose one sentence or phrase to reflect on for the week. Here are some ideas:

   - Because of Jesus Christ, God no longer holds my sins against me.

   - The uncompromising judgment of God is revealed in the suffering love of the cross.

   - When I forgive the person who has done me harm, giving up any resentment or desire to retaliate, I do not condone the harm that was done or excuse the evil of the sin.

   - I cannot love my enemies, I cannot pray for those who persecute me, I cannot even be ready to forgive those who have really hurt me, without the grace that comes from above.

   - When the great hope is truly alive, small hopes arise even now for alleviating the sufferings of the present time.

   - God does not will to be God without us, but instead grants to us creatures—fallen and mortal as we are—eternal life.

   - Heaven is our true home, a world of love.

See if you can memorize the sentence or phrase you choose, or at least remember the gist of it. Let this phrase stick with you through the week. Include it in your prayers, think about it while you are in the car, and remember it in the midst of a stressful situation. Look for connections between the phrase you selected and the world around you. Perhaps a conversation, a TV show, a current event, or a situation at home or at work will remind you of it. Record your thoughts and observations about this phrase and others in the journal space provided.

2. As you reflect back on this study, how has your faith been strengthened? Where have you found clarity in your understanding? What areas do you want to work on? How has your understanding of what it means to be a church member grown or changed?

_____

_____

_____

_____

_____

_____

_____

_____

_____

_____

_____

_____

_____

_____

_____

_____

_____

_____

_____

Where Will You Go from Here?

Congratulations! You have made it through the eight sessions of *Foundations of Faith*. You now have a greater understanding of the faith we confess and its implications for your life. Before you stash this guide in the back of a closet, take a few moments to evaluate your experience and decide where you will go from here.

What is one truth that you have learned in this class that you will take with you and never forget?

What habits of prayer, scripture reading, reflection, and action have you developed while working in this journal? Which of those do you want to continue? What new habits would you like to develop?

What will be the next step in your Christian education? Are there particular topics or areas you are interested in learning more about? Are there upcoming classes or Bible studies at your church that you would benefit from participating in?

How have you made new friendships or strengthened old ones during the group sessions?

What steps will you take to continue to develop those relationships?